signed

03/26/2012

To: Ann Marie
   &
   Kat

Thanks for being
the perfect host!!

John Moore

Alvetta

John C. Moore

iUniverse, Inc.
New York Bloomington

Alvetta

Copyright © 2008 by John C. Moore

All rights reserved. No part of this book may be used or reproduced by any means, graphic, electronic, or mechanical, including photocopying, recording, taping or by any information storage retrieval system without the written permission of the publisher except in the case of brief quotations embodied in critical articles and reviews.

iUniverse books may be ordered through booksellers or by contacting:

iUniverse
1663 Liberty Drive
Bloomington, IN 47403
www.iuniverse.com
1-800-Authors (1-800-288-4677)

Because of the dynamic nature of the Internet, any Web addresses or links contained in this book may have changed since publication and may no longer be valid. The views expressed in this work are solely those of the author and do not necessarily reflect the views of the publisher, and the publisher hereby disclaims any responsibility for them.

ISBN: 978-0-595-52092-3 (pbk)
ISBN: 978-0-595-62157-6 (ebk)
ISBN: 978-0-595-50864-8 (cloth)

Printed in the United States of America

Acknowledgements

I took on the task of writing a book at the same time my wife of over 50 years was coping with terminal brain cancer. It is the most difficult yet rewarding task that I have ever attempted.

I made a promise to my wife, Alvetta, that I would write this book and keep her name and memory alive. I always keep my promises.

I will tell you that I had to truly believe in God and ask that He provide me with the skill, patience, and support of family and friends to finish this book.

After helping me with my first book, "A Positive Attitude is a Muscle," my daughter, Audrey Madyun, told me "Dad, never again." I knew, however, when I told her of this project, that she again would champion the cause and do a lot of the heavy lifting. Without her help, this book would never have been completed.

As you will see when you read the book, many family and friends came to my aid in its creation. But a large number of strangers, professionals, volunteers and caregivers, provided me with cards, letters flowers and support during my darkest moments as well.

I will never forget the wonderful angels of Hospice of Northwest Ohio who truly became a second family.

Others who also surrounded me with their support and presence include the staff and faculty of Owens Community College, Charms, Inc. of Toledo, St. Joan of Arc Church and Third Baptist Church of Toledo, Delta Sigma Theta sorority, my Boulé brothers, St. Martin de Porres, and so many others.

I would also like to give thanks to Janet Hipp and Gary Corrigan for all of their help in the final draft.

A very special thanks goes to all of the caregivers of the world. You are not alone. God is watching—and He is with you.

Foreword

Working at Hospice of Northwest Ohio for the past 25 years, I have seen many patients and families receive our care. But when my phone rings and I hear the familiar voice of a friend—hesitant and hurting, asking for help—I am more mindful than ever of the magnitude of our responsibility.

In the fall of 2006, when John called to tell me Alvetta's prognosis and ask for Hospice care, I was sad but proud to offer our services. I knew our staff could guide the Moore family as they embarked on this inevitable journey. A top priority at this important time is to help patients and families identify goals they would like to accomplish. We were so pleased to see that Alvetta and John embraced their remaining time together and shared an end-of-life experience that was meaningful and fulfilling.

Until you have witnessed the illness and death of another person, you may not understand that caring for someone on Hospice is often a time of contrasts—a time that is physically and emotionally difficult but richly rewarding. During the months Hospice of Northwest Ohio cared for Alvetta, our staff was inspired and renewed as they witnessed on a daily basis the deep love and dedication of the Moore family. It was a profound privilege to care for Alvetta. We thank the Moore's for allowing Hospice of Northwest Ohio to play a small role during this significant time in their family's history.

Judy Seibenick, RN, BSN, Executive Director

Hospice of Northwest Ohio

A Simple Beginning

As I walked in the procession to the sound of "Lead Me, Guide Me", my mind flashed back to the very early life of my wife, Alvetta.

She was born in a small town in Alabama called Evergreen. Her mother and father moved to Toledo, Ohio before her first birthday. Her family was part of the migration north to find jobs. She would travel the world, but Toledo would always be home.

The family moved around Toledo until they moved into the Brand Whitlock apartment complex. This was federally funded and owned with rents based on family size and income. It was a city within a city. Its composition was made up of 375 model apartments and row houses with a park and playground facilities. Stores, doctors' offices, bars, grills and public schools surrounded it.

Alvetta lived in the heart of the projects as we called them. Her address was 320. This is where she would make friends that would last a lifetime. She would play, fight, and enjoy the life of a small child in a community that would all banded together to raise the children as if it were one large family with so many uncles, aunts, and cousins. She would live in this family community until she was 12.

My mind drifts back to the reading of the first scripture—Isaiah 25:6a 7-9. I could hear the reader saying "on this mountain the Lord of Hosts will provide for all peoples."

I closed my eyes and could see Alvetta at age 4 in her first days in a Catholic nursery school. Her mother would put Alvetta in a starched, well-pressed dress, grease her legs and face, braid her hair, and polish her white shoes or wash off the patent leather ones. This daily routine of being well-dressed and groomed would become a tradition with her that would last a lifetime.

The Catholic school and church that Alvetta attended was called St. Benedict de Moor. Located in the heart of the black community, it was school and church for most of the African-American Catholic population of that era. It was lost to a late 1960s expressway construction, but that is another story.

I remember asking Alvetta to write a little about her early days in the projects, in church, school and about her friends. The following is in her words, written over 25 years ago.

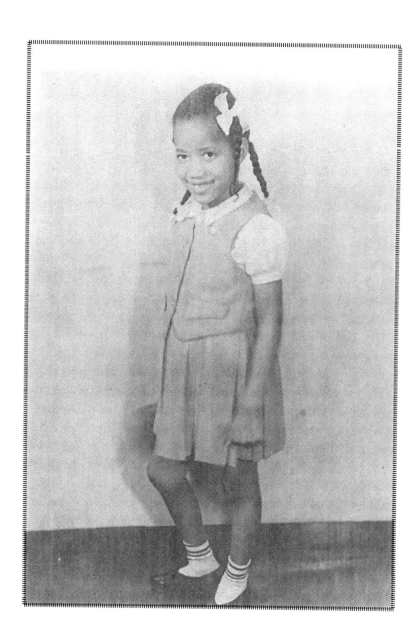

Alvetta's Story

"When thinking back to my childhood, my first thoughts are those of summer days filled with fun. I guess I am basically a summer-oriented person because the first signs of spring seem to ignite something within me. I had a good childhood with a loving family. My only regret was the fact that I did not have any brothers or sisters. That void has been filled with family and an abundance of friends.

My preschool days are very vague other than a few events during that period of time. I do remember parades, especially the parade in celebration of the end of World War II. There were soldiers in uniform marching and people on the sidelines cheering with joy. Just a few months before the end of the war came word that President Franklin D. Roosevelt had died. My parents, along with others, were saddened with this news. I did not really understand why they were so sad.

It was also during this period of time that my Uncle Clanford, who was in the army, sent me straw slippers from the Philippines. I suppose the memory of this gift lasted because it was from my favorite uncle whom I called "Uncle Wiggly,' a character from one of my childhood storybooks.

Clanford is my father's youngest brother from my grandfather's first marriage. He is the youngest of five children of my paternal grandparents, Frank and Allie Samuel Howard. After the death of my grandmother, (when my dad was thirteen years old) my grandfather remarried. From this union, came six more children.

I don't really know why this uncle was so special to me other than the fact he always let me tag along with him during my early years. I believe I was sort of special to him too, although I feel he never completely forgave me for growing up.

Elementary school days bring many memories, especially those of the Notre Dame nuns, who were very strict. It always amazed me that they were able to move about so freely while clothed from head to toe in what seemed to be heavy black fabric, contrasted by only a small stiff white collar and white accordion trim around the habit.

As for my first teacher, I guess I was as impressed with her as much as most first graders are with their first all-day teachers. Her name was Sister Mary Yvonne. Evidently I liked her very much because at this early age I decided that I should give myself the middle name Yvonne. Whenever anyone asked for my full name, my reply was "Alvetta Yvonne Howard." My mother must have accepted my determination on taking on this added name because when asked what my name by someone, she would answer "She says, it's Yvonne, but we didn't give the name to her."

The name is now considered legal, having gone to Washington D.C. on my passport application and being checked on various documents for its approval. My middle name has been passed on to two generations. First to our daughter, Cathy Yvonne, whom we lost two and a half years ago, and now to our granddaughter, our son's first born, Malayna Yvonne. She is presently thirteen months old.

There is also the memory of Father Joseph Shea, pastor of our parish, and dearly loved by all. I can recall the practice sessions for skits to be performed by students for Father Shea's feast day yearly. After having dressed in our Sunday best and performed for our pastor, fellow students and teachers, we were treated to a movie (Laurel & Hardy or something similar). When the program ended, there came the anxiously awaited news that we would have a free day from school the next day because we had all worked so hard.

It was also during these early years that I decided I would never eat peanut butter and jelly together on a sandwich. I had never eaten the two together anyway, but after this incident, I knew that I never would. It all started after one of the children tossed their lunch bag aside, only to be discovered by one of the nuns. When questions arose as to the owner of the lunch, someone told her it belonged to me. Right away, I denied ownership, having nearly completed my lunch saying, "My mother never packs me peanut butter and jelly sandwiches, because I don't like them." Well, Sister didn't accept my reply and she didn't seem to realize that I wouldn't lie to her for the fear that the devil would simply snatch me away if I had. She just insisted that I eat this sandwich, for which some starving pagan baby would love to have, or miss having after lunch recess with the other children. Needless to say, my determination took hold and I missed recess that day. There was a good feeling with me the next day as I handed her the note from my mother saying that the thrown aside lunch did not belong to me.

I often smile when I think of that incident, because having married a lover of peanut better and jelly sandwiches, I found myself making them often. The funniest part of all is the fact that I have now developed a taste for a peanut butter and jelly sandwich every once in a while.

There were also the years of playing with paper dolls, jacks, hopscotch, jumping rope, hide and seek and various other activities. Saturday morning cartoons were not watched on television, but attentively listened to on the radio. I recall some of the favorites as being Archie Andrews, Uncle John and Sparky, and the Buster Brown Show.

Sunday afternoon movies soon became a must. A lunch or brunch after attending Sunday Mass and my friend Janet Easterly and I were off to a downtown movie theater. Punishment of not being allowed to go to the movie was like the world coming to an end, so I did try to do what was expected of me to avoid this horrible alternative. I only remember once or twice not being allowed to go to the "show' on Sunday during this time. My mother always says I was a little stubborn, except when one of the nuns at school told me to do something (with the exception of eating the peanut butter and jelly sandwich).

These early school days were mixed with many extracurricular activities. There were piano lessons, but only for about a year. The violin lessons were for even a shorter period of time. This was probably because they were never by choice.

I'll never forget the Christmas Auntie Ann and Uncle Harold arrived with a huge gift, among others. I was so excited when I found out my name was on the big package. I just knew that the package had to contain a large doll, and never would have guessed that inside was a violin. I had enjoyed listening to my Uncle Harold play the violin on my visits to their home, and I appreciated the fact that he was known in the Toledo area for his playing in various supper clubs, but experiencing the pain of trying to hold the instrument under my chin was just not my idea of something I wanted to learn. Soon after, my cousin Donnie went to live with my uncle. He thought he would like to try his hand at playing the violin. I willingly turned my violin over to him, but for some reason, the lessons didn't last very long for him either.

During the summer of my 12th birthday, my parents moved from the area and the apartment complex where I had lived. We moved into the upper duplex of my Auntie Ann's and Uncle Harold's house. I was not there for the big move because I spent the summer in the south with my grandparents. That was an experience in itself because the lifestyle was so different.

This southern town in Alabama was my birthplace, but my parents moved to Toledo before I was a year old. As far as I was concerned, city life in Toledo was all I knew.

Although I basically stayed with my maternal grandparents, I also spent quite a bit of time with my paternal grandparents. They were both farmers with farms next to one another.

My mother's youngest sister, Cleo, had already moved to Toledo and was living with us and sharing my room. Cleo and I also share the same birthday (June 12th) and being 7 years older than me, she was somewhat like being a big sister.

The only child still at home with my maternal grandparents at this time was my mother's youngest brother James, who is five years older than me. Of course, I latched on to James as a big brother and he still refers to me as his "little sis". Whenever Mom's next oldest brother refers to me, as "our little sister" my mother's reply is, "Just how old do you think I am?"

All in all, just as I got a middle name, I found a way to get a sister and two brothers. The children of these two uncles and aunt—(James, Percy, and Cleo) have always referred to me as "Auntie Al" and I love it.

My paternal grandparents had six children still at home during this visit. As I mentioned earlier, these children were born of my grandfather's second marriage. Three were older and three were younger than me.

My grandparents on both sides were very loving and always seemed to cater to me on my visits, especially my grandfathers, who have both left me with some warm memories. The only one left is my maternal grandmother, who is now 87 years old and living here in Toledo.

The bright thing during those days was the trip to town for the day on Saturdays, where one enjoyed meeting with other family members and friends. Weekly grocery shopping was also done. I guess I'll always remember hearing my Granddaddy Frank saying, "Come on baby and go with granddaddy to the Piggly Wiggly", which was the name of the big supermarket.

Although lifestyles were different than what I was accustomed to, I can now look back and realize that it was a portion of my heritage and I had the opportunity to experience a different style of living.

The end of this summer vacation seemed to be the beginning of a new phase in my life. I returned from my trip to a new home, some soon to be new friends and the beginning of the adolescent age.

Friends Forever

Diane's Story

Today is Thanksgiving 2006. I have just left St. Martin de Porres Catholic Church for mass and I have come to the realization that God is going to take my sister-girlfriend to be with Him soon.

I have known this for sometime, but today at Mass, He whispered in my ear and told me to be prepared. The time is near.

I have tried to write a few stories about our very special friendship and I just can't—not right now.

Later.

I had moved to Toledo from New Orleans in 1948. I was the only colored kid in the neighborhood that was Catholic. The nearest Catholic Church was Polish and I was not welcomed to worship there. I had to go to St. Benedict's Catholic Church, which was quite a distance from my home. I walked six blocks and took a bus for the next half-mile to the Catholic Church that had been designated for the "Colored Catholics" in Toledo. Because of the distance, my Catholic education ended when I moved to Toledo.

It was August 15, 1951, the Day of Assumption, a Holy Day of Obligation for all Catholics. I was walking down Hawley Street to Dorr to take the bus to get to church. When I got to Avondale Avenue, two blocks from my home on Vance Street, a little girl was standing on the corner waiting for me. She said "Hi" and I answered "Hi". She asked if I was going to mass at St. Benedict's. I said yes and that is how this great friendship began.

When I think back, Alvetta and I were so much alike. We were about the same color in skin tone; we both had "long hair that didn't have to be straightened" (good hair); she had a light-skinned father and I had a light skinned mother; and we were Catholic. These were the things that made us a little different in our African-American neighborhood in 1951.

Our parents became friends, which just helped seal our very close friendship. We shared each other's friends and had a very good childhood. Today we still have those same friends. Alvetta and I are just a little closer.

Oh! The things we did together were as just as funny now as they were then. Here are just a few stories.

Alvetta "developed" earlier than I did and she teased me about it. At the time, Alvetta was in Catholic and I attended public school. Her school went on Easter break before mine did, and my mother took her shopping to get my Easter outfit. Alvetta helped pick out my very first bra, a satin one with a pink bow. Beautiful clothing and lingerie were important to Alvetta even then.

When I wanted Alvetta to spend the night and we thought Mrs. Howard would say "No", we had my baby sister call and ask, "Missy Howard, can Betta spend the night?" Cynthia was so cute and sweet that Mrs. Howard just couldn't say no.

Our mothers would really talk about us. Just because we didn't keep our rooms clean they said that they would need to keep balls of string in their purses to be able to find the way out of our dirty houses. Alvetta and I are very good housekeepers today and always have been even when we had small children. So, mothers, when the kids don't keep their rooms clean it doesn't mean that they aren't listening. They will be ok.

Of course, we weren't always the best kids and could be difficult when we didn't get our way. One time when Mrs. Howard said that Alvetta couldn't stay over, we were so upset we decided to run away from home. After we had gotten about three blocks with no plans as to where we were going and/or how we were going to survive, it started to rain. I can remember standing on the corner with Alvetta trying to decide which way to go. We finally decided we would give our parents one more chance to be better parents. We hugged and went home like good little girls.

Then came those teen years and boys! There is a picture of us at my house where Alvetta is talking to a boy on the phone and I am on her shoulder telling her what she needed to say.

Alvetta was to go with me to Chicago in the summer of 1955 for a vacation to visit my relatives. Well, that had to be cancelled because a relative of Alvetta's had decided to visit and Alvetta had to stay in Toledo to be with her "young aunt." I understand they went skating and Alvetta met John Moore. This meeting changed our lives completely. She had a serious "boyfriend"! Oh, I had had boyfriends too, but that was serious. They later married and John became my "brother". Of course, I was the maid of honor.

We both married young. Alvetta had two children, Cathy and Howard (Ric). I had four: Gary, Tanya, Moreatha and Veronica. I was godmother for Cathy. Alvetta and John were godparents to Veronica.

When Alvetta graduated from the University of Toledo with a Bachelor's in Education degree, I remember it was so hot in the stands that my mother kept busy drying my tears of joy and wiping the sweat from my face. I never did graduate from UT but I had a real education in life experience and had a very successful career in the business world.

Our lives took different paths but we always remained the best of friends. We were there for each other, through thick or thin, through good times and not-so-good times. Our friendship never waned.

I was born on October 31, 1938 and Alvetta was born on June 12, 1939. When we were young, I would tell her that I was the oldest and she would remind me that it didn't matter because we would vote at the same time. As we grew older, she would always smile when we disagreed and say, "But you are older than me."

Alvetta made her heavenly transition on June 11, 2007, the day before her sixty-eighth birthday. My gravesite is just a few feet from Alvetta's. So one day we will be neighbors again!

Diane T. Flaggs

The Most Beautiful Day of the Year

The words and music of Psalms 27 "The Lord is My Light and Salvation" brings me back from the past.

St. Joan of Arc is packed with family friends, coworkers, members of the church and a number of workers from Hospice of Northwest Ohio. I look around at all of the people. They smile, they cry, they are happy to see me—other heads are bowed. Although I feel pain, I know that the real pain of losing Alvetta has not yet been realized. It's going to very hard living without someone that you have shared everything with for almost 52 years—52 years.

My mind and soul leave the church again. This time it is July 24, 1954. It was the most beautiful day of the year. This was the day I met Alvetta Yvonne Howard. My mother's church had sponsored a hayride to Toledo Beach. I really did not want to go. We rode to the beach sitting on straw in two large trucks. In Alvetta's yearbook from Notre Dame Academy, I wrote, "We met on the most beautiful day of the year, July 24, 1954".

I was just returning from Arkansas after over four years and really did not know anyone except my family. My mother had to really talk me into going. The biggest thing to do at the beach was to roller skate, dance or swim and I was not good at roller-skating, dancing or swimming. So why go, I asked her. Mothers can talk their children into anything. The next thing I knew I was in the back of the truck with the wind in my face. I was watching this beautiful girl fighting to keep the wind from blowing her hair and she was losing. I offered my cap, which she refused. I asked my brother for his cap and he refused.

I really wanted to get to know her but she was not interested. I watched her dance and skate. After she finished, I walked over and introduced myself, pointing out my mother and brother. She said,

Alvetta

"I know your brother, but I do not know you and I do not talk to strangers."

I asked my mother to let Alvetta know that I was her son, and that I was ok to talk to. Alvetta had just turned 15 and I was 18. She finally told me her name—Alvetta.

I asked if she had a nickname. She said, "Yes, it is Alvetta Yvonne". She let me know right then and there that she did not like nicknames and if I could not call her by her given name, I could not call her by any other.

I told her my name was Johnny. I was born J. C. Moore. I did not know at the time that Alvetta had added "Yvonne" to her name and I would go from J. C. to Johnny to John and now I use both J. C. and John C. But, that's another story.

At the end of the day she was talking to me but barely. She gave me her telephone number as we rode back to Toledo.

I could not wait until the next day after work to call her. That was the beginning of our relationship. It was very slow for a few months. I did not think it was going to last. We were very different.

Alvetta was very quiet but outgoing. She was always well groomed and had a nice, refined quality about her. She loved the arts, movies, good books and great food. I was a kid who, for the last four years, had spent my spare time raising hogs, farming, hunting, fishing and camping. For the first couple of months I thought that we were two people that should not be together.

In my mind, she was refined and I was country. She knew how to dress—I loved my blue jeans. She knew classical music, the Old Masters and the greatest writers of all times. Could this relationship last?

The reader brought me back to the present reading words from Romans 8:14-23: "Those who are led by the Spirit of God are the Children of God." The reader's voice was strong and pulled me away from my thoughts of the past. As she finished up her reading she went on to say:

"We know that all creation is groaning in labor pains even until now, and not only that, but we ourselves who have the first fruits of the spirit; we also groan without ourselves as we wait for adoption, the redemption of our bodies." The Word of the Lord.

I looked around to see all of the people that had been a part of our 52 years and 11 months together. A part of our 51 years, and 7 months as husband and wife. I saw her old classmates, project friends and family from near and far. My best man at our wedding, her maid of honor. There were her mother and father, our children, grandchildren and great grandchildren. All were present for this day. All had shared with Alvetta and me the pain of a loved one's living with brain cancer.

Over the last 15 months, friends and family had sent over a thousand cards, numerous flowers, books, poems, and stories to share. They had sent food and prayed with us to help us hold on to our faith.

There were the ladies that she met at the YMCA, teachers she taught with, students she had taught, people from churches and other organizations throughout the community. All came to show how much she was loved, but mostly to say, "Goodbye, Alvetta".

The staff from Notre Dame Academy, her high school, classmates from St. Benedict's Elementary School, Members of Delta Sigma Theta sorority, her sewing club, staff from Hospice of Northwest Ohio, faculty and staff from the University of Toledo and Owens Community College, members of the Red Hat Society, Charms, Inc., and more! They all came to show their last respects to this wonderful lady we call Alvetta!

Hallelujah! Hallelujah! Hallelujah!

My mind will not stay in the present. It's November 5, 1955. Alvetta and I are exchanging vows in a small Catholic Church called St. Benedict's. She is 16 and I am 19. We are two very young kids ready to commit to a life together.

After the services and we had had time to be together, we talked about all the friends and family who'd told us our relationship would not last. They felt the odds were against us: lack of education, our young age, plus our religious and cultural differences. The list went on and on.

Early on, we made a promise to each other that I know was stronger than our vows. We promised each other that we would only be parted by death. We promised that we would forgive each other for our human weaknesses. God knows I had many then and now.

In the coming years, we made mistakes, yielded to temptation, broke our vows. However, we never did break our promise to each other to stay together. We suffered the loss of jobs, family and friends, but not the loss of each other.

Writing about two teenagers' first year of marriage could fill volumes. Alvetta had not finished high school and I had not gone to college. We had a baby on the way. I was starting to believe all of the negative predictions that this marriage was doomed from the beginning.

My small hourly wages could not really support us without the large number of things we had to give up. The day we married we started a budget that lasted for over 40 years.

I think we were the last of our generation to finally own a TV, buy a car or stereo, go on vacations, own the latest fashions and start having dinner "out".

Our rules were to pay the bills first and then go grocery shopping. Vacations were Sunday trips with the in-laws as we rode with them out into the countryside.

In later years, my in-laws joined in as Alvetta and I traveled the world.

Cookies and Ice Cream

I flash back to the present. The part of the gospel that helped me most was "Rejoice and be glad for your reward will be great in Heaven."

I know Alvetta is in Heaven and she is watching over me. I can remember many times in our life together she would say, "John, now it's my time to take care of you." I also know that Alvetta could always find joy--even at the worst times.

The first time I was laid off from the Iron Company, I was not yet 21 years old with a daughter and a wife to take care of. We were living from paycheck to paycheck with no savings of any kind and now I had no job! Alvetta had put aside a few dollars and went out to pick up our favorite dessert: oatmeal raisin cookies and a pint of black walnut ice cream. This does not seem like much but it was a feast to us! We rejoiced that we had each other! Over the years, at our darkest moments, one of us would take time to stop and pick up oatmeal raisin cookies and black walnut ice cream!

This was our way of letting the other know that no matter what was taking place at the time, that together we could handle it. In 52 years, we ate a lot of cookies and ice cream.

Father Hite's Homily

"On this mountain the Lord of hosts will provide for all peoples. On this mountain He will destroy the veil that veils all peoples. The web that is woven over all nations; he will destroy death forever.

The Lord God will wipe away the tears from all faces; the reproach of His people He will remove from the whole earth; for the whole earth; for the Lord has spoken.

On that day it will be said: "Behold our God, to whom we looked to save us! This is the Lord for whom we looked; let us rejoice and be glad that he has saved you!" The word of the Lord.

A reading from the Holy Gospel according to Matthew: When Jesus saw the crowds, he went up the mountain, and after he had sat down, his disciples came to him.

He began to teach them, saying;

> Blessed are the poor in spirit for theirs
> is the Kingdom of heaven
> Blessed are they who mourn, for
> they will be comforted.
> Blessed are the meek, for they will inherit the land.
> Blessed are they who hunger and thirst for
> righteousness, for they will be satisfied.
> Blessed are the merciful, for they will be shown mercy.
> Blessed are they clean of heart, for they will see God.
> Blessed are the peacemakers, for they
> will be called children of God.
> Blessed are they who are persecuted for the sake of
> righteousness for theirs is the Kingdom of heaven.

> Blessed are you when they insult you and
> persecute you and utter every kind of evil
> against you falsely because of me.
> Rejoice and be glad, for your reward
> will be great in heaven.

The Gospel of the Lord.

A reading from the letter of St. Paul to the Romans. Brothers and sisters:

Those who are led by the Spirit of God are children of God. For you did not receive a spirit of slavery to fall back into fear, but you received a spirit of adoption, through which we cry, "Abba, Father!" The Spirit itself bears witness with our spirit that we are children of God, and if children, then heirs, heirs of God and joins heirs with Christ, if only we suffer with him so that we may also be glorified with him.

I consider that the sufferings of this present time are nothing compared with the glory to be revealed for us.

For creation awaits with eager expectations the revelation of the children of God; for creations was made subject to futility, not of its own accord but because of the one who subjected it, in hope that creation itself would be set free from slavery to corruption and share in the glorious freedom of the children of God.

We know that all creation is groaning in labor pains even until now; and not only that, but we ourselves, who have the first fruits of the Spirit, we also groan within ourselves as we wait for adoption, the redemption of our bodies. The word of the Lord.

To you, John; to Alvetta's parents, Mary and Samuel; to your children, grandchildren and great grandchildren; all family members and friends who have gathered here to worship this morning, St. Joan of Arc Parish expresses our sincere sympathy and offers you the support of our prayers in this time of grief.

Life is the journey that has brought us here today as we surrender to the inevitability of death, particularly for someone like Alvetta who has struggled for a long time and courageously embraced the suffering the Lord has given her; this surrender, however, is not left without meaning.

To gather this morning for a Mass of Christian Burial celebrates Alvetta's and our belief that for those who have endured suffering, as Christ did, a new and eternal life is granted to the faithful servant.

As we turn to take comfort from each other, and as we listen to the Word of God proclaimed in this morning's Scriptures, perhaps we learn another lesson. And that lesson is that death does not have the final word! The Lord has promised us that a great reward awaits those who have been faithful and who have believed in his salvation.

So, as we listen to the words of the prophet Isaiah, we are given the vision of a *mountain.* It is salvation. It is fulfillment; it is peace. Isaiah says that the Lord God will wipe away the tears from our faces—that mourning and grief are short lived because our faith tells us that God will not abandon us. We are His children and His love for us is so great that He wants to share His life with us!

St. Paul, in his letter to the Romans, testifies that he himself has endured suffering for the sake of the gospel. And the suffering Paul experienced prompted him to write, "I consider the sufferings of the present to be **nothing** compared with the ***glory to be revealed for us!*** St. Paul was convinced-that because we are children of a living and merciful God—we are redeemed, and therefore will share in the glory of Christ as his sons and daughters!

And in that beautiful gospel that we just heard from St. Matthew, Jesus calls us to measure our years in terms of the things of God; in humble generosity to others, in mercy and forgiveness joyfully given, in a holiness strived for, in a justice won, in peace realized, in principles defended, in beliefs lived.

I have known Alvetta only for a few years. I had the joy of being introduced to her and John at a parishioners' home one evening. It was delightful. We all knew Alvetta to be a gracious lady. Quiet. Confident. Articulate. Considerate. Well, a teacher. I did not know she was known as "the Queen Mother" for the K.I.S.S. chapter of the Red Hat Society until I read her obituary. But yes, that was an appropriate title for her!

From the first she knew of her terminal illness, she accepted it gracefully.

I thank the Lord for the moments we shared when I would bring the sacrament of the Anointing of the Sick and Holy Communion to her. This faithful servant inspired **me** to keep **my** eyes focused on what was above! Her serenity, her will to live each day to the fullest, gave me strength and secured my faith.

But perhaps the best testament of her strength and devoted faith came when I visited her for the last time. I prayed with her; laid my hands upon her head; anointed her and said to her, "Alvetta, I wish that the Lord would heal you and restore you. I wish there was more I could do for you." And she responded, "He must have a reason."

She now knows His reason.

Each of us is given the task entrusted to the faithful servant. The reality of it is—some are given more time than others to accomplish that task. Alvetta's task was complete.

In gathering this morning, we trust in the Lord's mercy and love as He welcomes Alvetta into the joy of eternal life first promised her in baptism. Her passing is a reminder to all of us of the value of living and the satisfaction that comes from making each day count.

Above all, we thank God for the blessings He has given **us** in the life Alvetta shared. As we entrust her soul to the mercy of God's love, ***let our faith be renewed***—that each day that God gives us we may share His life, His hope, His joy with others, so that our world may be a better place for the human family.

Alvetta, all of us pray with you this morning, and may you share in the eternal banquet promised you from the day of your baptism. And may the words of our prayers for the commendation of the dying cause us to keep our eyes focused on the eternal life we hope to share with you some day.

"I commend you, my dear sister, to Almighty God, and entrust you to your Creator.

May you return to Him who formed you from the dust of the earth.

May Holy Mary, the angels, and all the saints come to meet you as you go forth from this life.

May Christ, who was crucified for you, bring you freedom and peace. May Christ, who died for you, admit you into His garden of paradise.

May Christ, the true Shepherd, acknowledge you as one of His flock.

May He forgive your sins, and set you among those He has chosen.

May you see your Redeemer's face to face and enjoy the vision of God forever!"

Family

As Father Hite finished his homily, my mind went to the early days before were married and how I was going to tell Alvetta about the coming births of two other children. When I finally told her we both cried and cried.

Years later, these two children and their children would become another of God's greatest gifts. Audrey and Alvetta were more like mother and daughter. Audrey's sons, our grandsons, loved their Nana and Grandnana (Alvetta's mother). It took years for Kevin, my other son, and I to find ourselves, but his daughter Nicole was truly as close to Alvetta as any of our other grandchildren.

Through all of this we truly witnessed the angel called Alvetta. I know that I will write future books and one of them will be on all of the children of John and Alvetta.

What a Trip!

After Father Hite's homily, Audrey and I had to carry the gifts as the church got ready for communion.

As we carried the gifts, my mind went back to my last trip to Florida with Alvetta. We left at the end of February with Alvetta's mother and father (Nana and Gramps). Our son Ric and his wife Shanon, their daughter Kyla and Audrey would join us later.

I knew something was wrong with Alvetta back in November, but I thought it was the stress of her parent's aging. She was changing. She was quick to get angry, worried constantly and bought clothes she did not need. She began to lose things in the house and forget appointments. I thought it could also be her own aging process.

After arriving in Florida and unpacking, like always, our next step was to the grocery store to stock up for our month's stay in Florida. I knew Alvetta had a problem then not only by the type of food we bought but the quantity. We bought so much food! At the end of this first grocery run, we had three carts of food for just four people.

We were ok the first week, but during the second week after the children arrived, she really changed. She was eating large amounts of food and did not want to leave the bedroom.

I finally took her out to play golf. She was so confused on the course that it frightened me.

The next day I took her for a massage, hoping it would make her feel better. After the massage, the attendant asked me to help my wife put on her clothes. She appeared to be having a problem getting dressed. At first Alvetta refused my help, but the attendant asked me again to get her dressed and out of the room as others were waiting. I went into the small dressing room and had to dress her. I knew then that we had a problem.

We returned to the villa and I explained to the family what had happened. They thought she was having a nervous breakdown. I told them I would call her doctor and tell him what had happened. Our doctor, back in Toledo, was deeply concerned. He thought Alvetta had had a mild stroke and asked me to take her to the nearest hospital.

On the 11th day of our winter vacation, I took Alvetta to a small hospital outside of Davenport, Florida. They ran test after test, and did a CT scan. Later that night they told her it could be a brain tumor. After Alvetta checked in, it was up to her mother and me to tell the family that Alvetta had a tumor.

The children had to return to Toledo to their jobs—leaving the four of us just as we had started: Nana, Gramps, Alvetta and me.

Three days later, the doctor told me that Alvetta had a brain tumor called Glioblastoma Multiforme (GMB). She would need surgery. I had never heard the term before, but knew people with brain tumors that survived and lived great proactive lives. Despite the working diagnosis, I knew Alvetta was strong and felt she would survive.

We were then told that the surgery had to be performed in Orlando at M. D. Andersen Cancer Center, which is a part of Orlando Regional HealthCare. The hospital was just a few miles away and we felt they would take Alvetta in just a few days.

Well, it was more than just a few days before the center had a spot for Alvetta. During this time, she was in great spirits, but was scared just like the rest of us about the upcoming procedure.

At last it was time to go. The day before, I had driven Nana and Gramps to the Center to make certain of the distance and location. I was glad that I did. I was not able to keep up with the ambulance and the traffic was awful.

It took them a few more days before surgery. The staff at the Center was excellent. I knew that Alvetta would have the best of care.

So, each morning for several days, I would pack Nana and Gramps in the car and head for the Center where we'd stay until dark and then head back to the villa. On the 5th day the doctor said that they were ready to operate and would let me know the results as soon as possible.

I was heartened to be told by the staff that Alvetta's doctor was one of the best in the country and she was in good hands.

I prayed with Nana and Gramps to make certain that God would guide this doctor's hands with skill and wisdom and that all illness be removed. I prayed that Alvetta would be herself once more.

Through good times and bad, all through our married life, I thought my job was to take care of Alvetta. We faced the best and the worst together. We had the same problems that all married couples faced. It's hard to explain to others, but even though Alvetta was smarter than me, it was my job to take care of her. And I did, but all of a sudden I felt so helpless.

There was no one that I could call upon in higher office (except God), no elected official, no TV station or friends to make things better. Had that been the case, I would have no worries, as I am good at networking and resolving problems. But this was a problem I could not solve. So I did what I could: I prayed. I prayed like I had never prayed before in my life.

Surgery was finally over and the doctor pulled me aside from Nana and Gramps and told to me what he had found. He explained the results of the operation, the treatment to follow and the prognosis: **Alvetta had six months to live**.

I almost passed out. I told the doctor that I wouldn't tell Nana and Gramps yet. I wanted to discuss this with Alvetta first after we were back in Toledo.

He confirmed the working diagnosis of GMB (Glioblastoma Multiforme), which was an aggressive type of primary brain tumor. She would need chemotherapy and radiation. This would not be a cure, but it would lengthen her life and the quality of it. He also told me that additional surgery would be of little or no benefit.

I kept this information to myself for a long time. I thought hope and prayers would make things better.

Finally I got to see Alvetta for a few moments. She was still sedated, but squeezed my hand after hearing my voice. Then Nana was allowed to visit. She cried. I cried. Alvetta's head was completely bandaged.

I told Nana that the tumor had been removed and we had to wait in Alvetta's room until she was ready to come out of recovery.

Kyla, Ric, Shanon and Audrey had returned home to Toledo by then. I called to tell them the outcome of the surgery, but I did not go into great detail. I told Audrey that it was Glioblastoma and she knew exactly what it was and the prognosis. I made her promise not to discuss that part with anyone until we returned to Toledo, but to let the family know that the tumor had been removed and I was waiting on the doctors to tell me if and when I could take Alvetta home.

My first task was to talk Nana and Gramps into going home. My hands were full. I was going to need all of my strength just to care for Alvetta.

Audrey and I talked about flying them home. They fought us, but I finally convinced them it was for the best. Nana did not want to go, but she had to. Gramps didn't look well and Nana was his caregiver. A few days later, after convincing them that Alvetta was out of danger, I put them on a plane to fly home toward the end of March.

Each day, I would drove from Davenport to Orlando and stay with Alvetta until she was really to go to sleep and I would then drive back to an empty villa. I was busy each night calling family and friends to update them. Two questions were asked over and over: "How is she doing? "Can I help you get her home?"

Finally, I met with the medical team. I told them that we were from Toledo. At first they wanted us to stay in Florida for Alvetta's follow up treatment. I told them I would provide her with any type of transportation they deemed necessary but we were going home.

With the help of a very professional social worker, we worked out the details. We could not take a train, plane, bus or ambulance. The best way would be for me to drive the 1,100 miles from Davenport to Toledo. We left on April 2. On April 8, Alvetta sent this email out to family and friends.

> From: AY Moore (aymoore@accesstoledo.com)
> To: Undisclosed recipients
> Sent: Saturday, April 8, 2006 7:59 p.m.
> Subject: What a Trip!

"For those of you who may not have heard or heard something that was not correct: this is from the horse's mouth.

John and I left Toledo Feb 26, 2006 heading for Florida for some R&R for the month of March as we did last year. We decided to take Mom and Dad with us so that we would not be down there worrying about them. The kids (Ric and his family and daughter, and Audrey, came to visit on the 14th). Audrey was to be there only four days because of her job, but Ric, Shanon and the baby had plans to stay a week. After a couple of days, Audrey and John decided that I was not myself and called the doctor back home. They were told to maybe take me to the ER in Florida, because I may have had a mini-stroke or something. Well, it turned out to be something.

After having an MRI, CT scan and an EEG, they determined that I had a brain tumor and would need surgery. My doctor felt that I should have it done down there. I was transferred to another hospital where they did that type of surgery and so on and on. I think I was hospitalized 11 days in all. They said I could only travel home by car or train. John wanted to drive me back and promised he would stop at least every 2 hours and walk me a little. We made it back Tuesday, April 4, 2006 and what a relief. It was all so very scary. I had asked different ones for prayer and could feel the prayers being poured down upon me.

I continue to have a long way to go and will continue to need prayers. I am going to be taking radiation and chemotherapy and have been informed that it may be a rough journey.

PLEASE keep me in your prayers and also John. He is being just wonderful taking care of me and sometimes being overprotective."

Alvetta

The Journey Begins

April 2, 2006. At 9:30 a.m. Alvetta and I left Davenport Florida, and started the 1,100 miles home. Alvetta just had major surgery. I had two secrets that I was not ready to share with her. One was about the cancer and the other was about the journal I had started.

For some, 1,100 miles is just a day trip of about 20 hours. We normally did it in 2 days but this time I had promised that I would take my time and stop often.

This was the worst and best time of our married life. We talked during all of her waking hours. We talked about the good and the bad. We talked about the pain, the sins, the forgiveness, the jobs and the celebrations we'd had. We talked about the children, their children and their children. She talked about secrets she'd kept from me, some of which were very painful. I talked to her about the secrets I'd kept from her.

Our love grew in this 1,100 mile journey. We had to stop almost every two to three hours. I had to help Alvetta to the restroom. Once, I had to go inside the stall with her. I bolted the door and cleaned her up. What a surprise we gave the ladies as we walked out of the ladies' restroom! Once we got to the car we laughed so hard that it hurt her.

We talked about the purchase of our first home. It was a 2-story, 3 bedroom and 1 bath house with a large kitchen and large backyard. Now, one must remember that what we thought was large then would be very small today.

I was 21 years old and Alvetta was 18. She was not of legal age to sign the paperwork. I had to become her legal guardian with the consent of her father. Now, this made her father, Gramps, very upset. He told me that he gave up his daughter once, but could not understand why he had to do it again!

Our first home became the gathering place for family dinners, birthdays, sleepovers and meetings. The smell of certain foods still takes me back to our first home. At that time Cathy and Howard (Ric) were the only two children in our lives.

During this time, Alvetta completed her high school education and became a secretary at the welfare department. I was working at a steel mill and taking a few college courses. It took every penny we had to meet the mortgage payments, buy food and such, but we did it.

It's funny looking back at how two young people were able to balance a budget, save a few dollars, send their children to private school and purchase a home on nickels a day.

One day we asked each other, "Do you like your job?" "Do you want to do this kind of work for the rest of your life"? We both answered, "No!" So we started to make plans to move on.

Alvetta had made up her mind that she wanted to teach. In order to do this, she had to go to college part time.

At age 31, Alvetta became a teacher. She obtained a Bachelor's degree in education and a Master's degree as well. Alvetta taught school for over 25 years.

The school administration had seen great potential in Alvetta and wanted to move her into an administration position. She refused and continued to do what she loved, but that's another story.

During our trip home, we talked about her teaching days, the students, teachers, parents and principals. Simply put, Alvetta loved teaching and was great at it. I wish now that I had kept her collections of letters from parents and students on the positive effect she had in their lives.

The education system started to change and the stress on teachers increased. Alvetta did not like what was happening in the public school system. After 25 years, it was time to enjoy her retirement.

It was quite an adjustment for her. She joined the YMCA. She took swimming classes, Tai Chi, frequented the gym and attended long luncheons with other ladies. Alvetta also got more involved in arts and crafts, her community and her many clubs. Her hunger for travel increased. These were just some of the reflections we had on our long journey home.

We talked about my career in banking. We talked about how I'd applied for a janitorial position and 25 years and 18 promotions later, I was a corporate vice president, but that's another story.

We talked about Kevin (my son) and his family and how we were becoming closer. We talked about how Nikki, Kevin's daughter, was as close to us as any of our other grandchildren. Alvetta started to cry when she recalled the times when Nikki began to call her Nana and Audrey started calling her Mom.

We talked about all of our travels with others and the ones we wanted to do on our own. She really got excited talking about the many adventures we had with the children, grandchildren and great grandchildren.

We talked about the wonderful trips she had with the Delta Sigma Theta sorority and Charms, Inc. She loved her 'sisters" and they truly were her sisters. She would finish one trip and start making plans for the next.

Alvetta talked about the time she started a chapter of the Red Hat Society called KISS, which stands for Kind, Intelligent, Savvy Sisters. We talked and talked until she fell asleep. I thanked God for those precious moments as I drove home to Toledo.

I am back in the present at St. Joan of Arc. The words of the Eucharistic Prayer bring me back. The church is really into the prayer. All heads are bowed and I know that it is a great time to pray for one's needs. I asked God to take care of Alvetta and to give us the strength to go on. I prayed for help for her parents. Parents are not supposed to outlive their children. As I prayed, my mind again slipped back to the first day of our 1,100 mile trip from Florida to Ohio.

We stopped every two to three hours. I would check her bandages and help her to the rest room. She would drink a little water, have a small snack and we'd be off again. Back on Route 75 we'd start talking once more about our life together.

We relived our many trips and vacations--first cruise, Alaska, Mexico, Switzerland, Canada and especially our wonderful trip to Italy. We recalled who went with us and the things we did, but our best trips ended up being the ones we took by ourselves. We laughed about how, in our early days, our "big trips" were to Detroit and Dayton to spend time with relatives, and our "big ventures" were the ones when we drove to Fordyce, Arkansas.

Our parents were scared for us on our first long trip. That was in 1959. Ric was still in diapers. Its funny how once we got the bug to travel, we never lost it.

Alvetta loved planning trips; she loved the Caribbean, Hawaii and Mexico. She loved shopping with a passion and the two went hand in hand. Alvetta also enjoyed Broadway, so we tried to visit New York at least once a year. We'd shop, take in at least three plays and find a new place to eat or a nightspot with great music. It's hard to believe what we accomplished in our years together.

At the end of the first day, we had traveled about 400 miles and Alvetta was exhausted by the time we got a room for the night. I helped her clean up, get comfortable and went to get a carryout dinner of soup, sandwiches and fruit. Alvetta immediately went to sleep.

I called Audrey to update her on our progress. I felt if I could get in 400-500 miles the following day, we'd complete the trip in 2 ½ days' time. I asked Audrey to let friends and family know that all was ok but that Alvetta did not need visitors the first few days.

I made up my mind that I would get another opinion before giving Alvetta all the facts about her cancer. This was hard. I was keeping a secret from her but suspected she already knew.

Back to the present. The choir was singing Blessed Assurance. "Blessed Assurance Jesus is Mine." This was one of Alvetta's favorite songs. Our newfound choir, led by Clarence Smith and friends with help from St. Martin de Porres and St. Joan of Arc, must have known it was one of Alvetta's favorites. Their voices were perfectly pitched and the majestic music filled the sanctuary. I knew that Alvetta was able to hear them sing and would have praised and sung with them. It is times like this that I know GOD is Real!

The entire church was now caught up in the moment and as the choir sung that last verse:

> Perfect submission, all is at rest
> I in my Savior am happy and blest,
> Watching and waiting, looking above,
> Filled with His goodness, lost in His love.

It was now time the signing of the book of Saints. Our two grandchildren, Nicole and Na'im walked together to the altar to write Alvetta's name in the book. As they walked to the altar, my mind went back to a little over a year ago—the second day of our 1,100 mile journey home.

The Pajama Party

I woke early after a very restless night hoping that I could make good time and not be too tired. Alvetta could be called a morning person, but not one to move in a hurry. At 7:30 a.m. she woke up, smiled, turned the TV on and slowly walked into the bathroom to prepare for the day. Since retiring, it generally took 2 $^{1/2}$ hours from the time she awoke until the time she'd be ready, so I knew I'd be in for a wait. I packed her clothes, made coffee and waited. She was in no hurry to get moving. So I went out and bought a huge breakfast and brought it to the room. By 10 a.m. we were on the road just north of Atlanta with 700 miles to go.

Alvetta revealed that she knew more about her cancer than I thought. She began to tell me about things we should think about. How she wanted to see her granddaughters, Brittney and Malayna. How she wanted to see her two great-grandsons, Christian and Andersen, as soon as possible. How we needed to decide what gifts she wanted to give away. And then she brought up a pajama party.

Alvetta wanted to throw an old-fashioned 1950s-style pajama party and invite some of her friends from around the country. She wanted to do this on her birthday and buy each one a gift. She told me all of the details including how she wanted Audrey and me to do the cooking and preparation.

With a hint of sorrow, she said she regretted that none of the children carried her name "Alvetta" and that it would die with her. I promised her that her name would never die. She looked at me straight in the eye and said, "OK, Mr. Miracle Worker. What are you going to do now?" I told her that starting that night I would begin writing a book about her.

She did not think it was a great idea and wondered under her breath who would buy it. I told her I would publish it myself and give copies to family and friends. She smiled then and said, "Good luck."

That night, I started putting notes together and for the next 20 months I worked on this book called "Alvetta". I knew in the beginning I could not cover her life or even our lives together in great detail. But I knew that I could attempt to hit the highlights.

We had so many highlights and so much joy, hope, pain, despair and happiness that it would take three volumes to cover it all. I did not know how I was going to write this book but I told Alvetta that I would and knew right then that I'd keep my promise.

Later that night, April 3, 2006, I called Audrey and gave her the update. I told her about the pajama party and asked her to start planning as Alvetta's birthday was just a couple of months away.

By 6 p.m. that evening we had covered another 400 miles. I told Alvetta that if we got a good start the next morning we could be home by 4 p.m. She said she'd be ready. Members of the family in Dayton wanted us to stop on the way home so they could see her for a few moments. I let them know that Alvetta needed to get home and sleep in her own bed. Except for rest and food stops, we would not be stopping.

At exactly 4 p.m. on April 4, 2006 we pulled into our driveway in Holland, Ohio, a suburb of Toledo. I called Audrey to come and assist me. I unpacked the car, put up our luggage and went to the grocery store while Audrey stayed with Alvetta.

A new chapter was beginning in our lives. Words like Glioblastoma Multiforme, primary brain tumor, malignant, CT scan, MRI, radiation therapy, chemotherapy and temozolomide, were added to our everyday words. The list went on and on.

Our family doctor referred us to one of the very best specialists in Toledo. After Alvetta rested for a couple of weeks, we went to see the specialist who had reviewed her medical history. I knew the doctor and his reputation. I had served on the board of Hospice of Northwest Ohio with him.

He went into great detail with us about Alvetta's tumor. Audrey printed up a sheet for the family that explained in great detail what he told us and what we had learned.

There are two types of glioblastomas, primary and secondary. Primary means that it started in the brain and secondary means that it came from elsewhere in the body. Mom has primary, and it has not spread outside of her brain.

One type, Glioblastoma Multiforme (GBM) is the most malignant. It rarely spreads outside of the brain, but grows rapidly and develops "tentacles" throughout the brain.

Glioblastomas are generally treated with palliative care (reducing symptoms and improving the quality of life rather than curative) and includes surgery, radiotherapy, and chemotherapy.

Without therapy, patients with GMBS die in 3-6 months. Those treated aggressively with surgery and other treatment live an average of 12 months.

The doctor then set up appointments for Alvetta to start her chemo and radiation in a few weeks. Alvetta and I got back in the car and cried like babies. All hope was now gone—this truly was the beginning of the end.

It would be a while before chemo and radiation would begin, so we planned a few trips together to Michigan and Canada just to get Alvetta out of the house for a few days. She was still weak and was unsteady when she walked. She had problems with her bladder. We had company everyday and invitations to all kinds of social engagements, which we turned down for the most part.

In a few weeks, Alvetta began to feel better. She wanted to go to our former church. She had previously asked a group at St. Martin de Porres to pray for her and she told me she felt their prayers and wanted to go to church and thank them.

That Sunday morning she put on a beige silk two-piece dress with matching shoes, perfect makeup and a scarf to cover her head. She looked like a model and her face was all aglow. She was the picture of perfect health and a great attraction at the church. When it was time for announcements, Alvetta walked up front and thanked the parishioners all for the prayers, gifts, and cards. She was their star that day.

We stayed at the church for the social gathering and were constantly surrounded. They told her how beautiful she was and how they loved her dress. Alvetta did not look as if she'd ever been sick. This would be her last visit to her beloved St. Martin de Porres.

Alvetta wanted to repeat the same appearance with other groups. I did not know it at the time, but she wanted to tell all of her friends goodbye. So, she met with her YMCA swimming ladies, her Deltas, her Charms, her Sew-N-So's, and her Red Hats.

She also wanted to meet a group from the "Y" that had become our friends. These were three couples that took turns hosting parties for the others with gourmet foods and fine wines. When it would be our turn, Alvetta would always invite 15 to 20 other couples over. She would prepare the side dishes, Audrey would do a fancy new dessert and I would grill. What a party!

We got together quarterly. Later that summer we received an invitation from the next event's host and hostess. Alvetta told me that we would go.

The couple's back yard led down to a large pond, which Alvetta loved. Again, she was the star. We all gave her our full attention. She enjoyed the wonderful food, wine, the water and the sun, but most of all, the company. This would be our last gathering with this group.

Alvetta really wanted to have her pajama party. She had put together a list of family and friends to invite. She wanted to have them all stay overnight and the ones from out of town could stay a few nights. She let Audrey select theme decorations, but she had in mind what she wanted to give for gifts.

Alvetta was getting a little weaker and unsteady from her treatments, but she was determined to find what she wanted. Alvetta was always the perfect shopper and a woman of great taste. I knew her gifts would be unique and special. We stopped at The Chocolate Shop outside of Toledo where she purchased boxed gourmet chocolates and specialty tea and holder sets for her guests. Inside each custom gift bag was a note saying, "Thanks for helping to lift my spirits and also for celebrating my birthday—I love you, Alvetta."

Later, Alvetta managed to climb the steps upstairs to her office where she made personalized invitations for each of her guests.

The big day finally arrived. The house was ready with 50s themed decorations and music. Under Alvetta's directions, we had the food and wine ready. Every available space in the house was stocked with extra towels, portable beds and toiletries.

The ladies arrived, some in their PJs, some ready to change. There was only one house rule: only Alvetta was allowed to go to sleep. All I could think of was getting out of there, but since Alvetta wanted me to stay, I huddled in our bedroom and checked in every hour or so. They danced, played cards, joked and reminisced. They ate. Gosh, did they eat. Audrey and I had bought and prepared lots of food and many of them ate and drank almost until dawn.

As Alvetta finally got ready for bed at 1 a.m., I could tell that she was tired, but very pleased that her party was a success. It would take me days to cleanup and months to restock the bar, but oh! What a party!

~A Time for All Seasons~

The summer of 2006 was coming to an end. The effects of Alvetta's treatment were having an increased number of side effects such as swelling, increased appetite and waning coordination.

I watched her very closely but by the fall, she had fallen a few times and needed more help than I could provide. So I asked a visiting nurse to come in three days a week to help with her medication, hygiene and exercise.

I found I was not satisfied with one of the doctors assigned to Alvetta. So I had her assigned to someone else. I felt better, but now I know it was not the doctor, it was me. I had to finally accept that Alvetta was dying. I was helpless and frightened. I was frightened for her, frightened for the family, but mostly frightened for myself.

I had shared most of my life with Alvetta. We faced all odds and we won, but now we faced another challenge. I knew that we could not win this one for I truly believed in Ecclesiastes 3, 1-2: To every thing there is a season, ….a time to be born, and a time to die……… Alvetta's office was on the second floor of our home. She had her arts and crafts, sewing and music in this room. This was her "space" and she would climb upstairs and stay for hours. Now she was too weak to climb the stairs so we got her a laptop computer to use downstairs. She could not seem to concentrate or stay focused long enough to use it and it was put aside.

Thanksgiving was coming. At one doctor's visit, we were advised that the tumor had returned and that we needed to start looking into Hospice care. When we returned home from this visit, Alvetta decided that we would make the upcoming Thanksgiving the best one ever. I was to tell "her girls", Nikki, Shanon and Audrey, that they were to prepare their best holiday dishes. I was to roast a turkey. In the past, I would grill it with a special barbeque sauce. So I began working on a new recipe for roasted turkey. Later the family told me that it was one of the best.

We had a full house at Thanksgiving: Nana, Gramps, children, grandchildren and greats, cousins and friends. We had so much food that it was a feast for the eyes before it was a feast for our stomachs. Not only did we have turkey and dressing and all the trimmings--everything was made from scratch—from the rolls, to the cranberry sauce to the many sides and desserts.

Although weak, Alvetta had an excellent appetite due to the steroids. After we'd sung songs, told stories and watched television, she took aside her "girls" and told them she was proud of them. In the past, she would do most of the cooking. Now they had stepped in for her and done well. She had passed on the torch. It was a wonderful, wonderful Thanksgiving.

The following week, Hospice of Northwest Ohio came to our home to evaluate Alvetta's needs. She could no longer bathe herself. She stumbled more often. She had recently slipped and damaged her toes so badly that she almost lost three of them. Her blood sugar readings were extremely high. I was afraid to leave her alone.

Earlier, Audrey had begun to come over on Sundays to relieve me. I would take in a movie, go shopping, and play golf. One particular Sunday, I was at the movies and felt something was wrong. As I walked in the door, I knew we had some decisions to make.

Alvetta's blood sugar readings had been high, due in part to the high doses of steroids and her increasing appetite. She would finish a meal and be hungry for the next one. While the steroids were helping the brain swelling and other problems, they were not good for her diabetes and had tripled her appetite so much that she would sneak food when she could. By now, we had a walker and a wheelchair for her. But Alvetta tried hard to remain the independent woman that she'd always been and would avoid assistance of any kind.

This particular Sunday morning, I got her up, bathed and got her breakfast ready like always. She took her meds and insulin and smiled her gracious smile when Audrey arrived. She was going to the bathroom frequently and was becoming increasingly incontinent. While I was gone, Audrey had a difficult time getting her to use the walker. She did not want Audrey to stay in the bathroom with her, so Audrey would help her to the bathroom, give her the supplies she needed and get her seated. She would stand by the door until called and would help Alvetta to the sink and then out. During one of these times, Audrey heard a large crash. Alvetta had fallen, trying to reach down under the sink on her own.

She fell and blocked the door so that Audrey couldn't get in. Alvetta was disoriented and it took her a long time to understand that she needed to roll over. Finally, Audrey got in but Alvetta couldn't understand how to follow her instructions to get up. When Audrey wanted her to lean, she would pull away.

Hospice had prepared us for such an eventuality. A quick call to them and paramedics were on their way. It took three paramedics to get her into a wheelchair, as Alvetta could not help them or herself. Her blood sugar readings were off the chart, well over 500. Normal is 100. Our blood sugar machine then malfunctioned. Thank God for friends, family and Hospice. In less than an hour, one neighbor had purchased a new blood sugar machine, another had brought communion, a Hospice nurse had made a visit, and Audrey and Hospice had worked out a plan for two night nurses to help me with Alvetta throughout the night.

The three of us—two nurses and myself, worked through the night. Although they were professionals, they had to get me to help them get Alvetta out of bed. They gave her insulin throughout the night but were able to get her blood sugar down only into the 300s. By morning, we were all exhausted. Throughout her illness, I had demanded the best of care for Alvetta and knew that I could no longer provide it at home.

The decision was made to move her into the Hospice facility. On December 3, Alvetta and I met with family and told them it was time to move into Hospice. The family did not want to accept Alvetta's condition or that Hospice was the right place. I again gave them a copy of a handout of Alvetta's cancer and explained to them, with Audrey's help, the need for Hospice. I also gave them a handout about Hospice of Northwest Ohio with this information.

Hospice of Northwest Ohio provides care and services to patients who are terminally ill. Hospice care and services focus on support and comfort to the patient and family, rather than curative care and treatment. Should the patient choose curative treatment, he or she is not eligible to receive Hospice services.

Hospice proves care and services to patients and families based on an interdisciplinary team approach. This means that, together with the patient and the family, the Hospice Plan of care is developed by all of the Hospice care providers who are involved with the patient and family, either directly or indirectly.

The goals of Hospice care are: to keep the patient comfortable; to keep the patient safe, to assist the patient to have sell-determined life closure, and to assist the patient and family to experience effective grieving.

This flyer, call the "Hospice of Northwest Ohio Information Fact Sheet" went on to explain the services available, the Medicare Hospice benefit, and that fact that this particular Hospice was a nonprofit organization.

As a caregiver and a selfish one, I realized the challenges, frustrations and loneliness of the task ahead of me. I did not want to share Alvetta with anyone. It was my responsibility to take care of my wife and I did not want to give that task to others.

The decision was overwhelming. I felt guilty at times and felt that it was my fault my wife was sick. There were times that I asked God to let me trade places with her. I pleaded with God and begged for answers, "She is such a good person, why is she dying like this?"

Everyday someone would hand me some reading material or mail me an article to help me at just the right moment. The "Care for the Caregiver" brochure from the American Brain Tumor Association really helped me. It started off saying that being a caregiver can be one of the most challenging but rewarding experiences a person can have. That I already knew. The brochure stated that a caregiver must:

1. Be kind and patient with yourself.

2. Assess what you need and seek resources (people, organizations and information) which can help meet your needs.

3. Take care of your own physical and health needs.

4. Take care of your emotional needs.

5. Decide to "do one thing today".

6. Be flexible.

7. Laugh.

In my need to do it all, I had forgotten that my need to do so was selfish. I had forgotten the primary goal—to have the best for Alvetta. I had forgotten that taking care of my own needs would help me be a better caregiver to Alvetta. Ever so often when I felt at my lowest, a friend or family member would provide me the information, kind word, or help that was needed. I knew that God was watching not only over Alvetta, but me as well.

A Bushel of Love

A Granddaughter's Story

Nikki--We started having Sunday dinner at Granddad's more often after Nana got sick. One Sunday, Nana called Shanon, Audrey and me together and told us she wanted us to prepare Thanksgiving dinner. Somehow I ended up with the greens and dressing. Corey and I had been married for a few years and our son Christian was still a little baby. Even though there were just two of us to cook for, I would always make so much we'd have leftovers for days. So, I went ahead and bought greens, thinking that with 10 folks for dinner, I'd better cook plenty. I bought and bought until I had a bushel of greens. I cooked and cooked and cooked. When I was done, I realized I had cooked too much and left part of the greens at home. Still when I got there, everyone kept asking me if I was trying to feed an army. Nana was happy, though. I guess I wanted to show her how much I loved her by trying to do what she asked. She had always been there for me through the many difficult times I'd had in the past.

It was hard visiting Nana in Hospice and sometimes I felt really bad. Christian and I went as often as I could. Nana was always happy to see us, especially Christian. We can say "I love you", in many ways, and I guess I did it with the bushel of green I cooked for our last Thanksgiving together.

Corey's Reflections

Corey--I simply remember the first time I met my now heavenly Grandmother-in-law: at a Christmas concert at an area parish with my then - fiance's Grandfather. It was a great, inviting place to meet new friends and family, and that's exactly what happened. What a warm place to be acquainted! The familiar feel of family and her warm smile is all it took to erase any formalities. From then on, Nana and Granddad were no longer in-laws, simply family.

Nicole (Nikki) and Corey Robinson

Milestones and Reflections

I had so many flashbacks during this final Saturday, June 16th 2007 at Alvetta's funeral services. None, however, were as vivid as our 1,100-mile trip from Davenport, Florida to back home in Toledo. As I look back over our life together, I can truly state that our greatest love affair took places during those 1,100 miles. We talked, laughed, confessed, shared and made plans. We came as close as two people could come together. I learned more about life, living, love and the fear of dying during this trip than I had in the 70 years before. I also discovered how selfish human beings could be.

We want more—even when we have enough. We glorify the wrong things. We fail to see our blessings. We blame the world for our shortcomings. We concoct stories to bring down others. We want the biggest houses, cars and paychecks. We create conflict and disagreements.

In this long journey I learned a lot about our truest needs and how much faith we must have in each other and God.

Wars, profits, crimes, keeping up with the Joneses and climbing the corporate ladders are really not that important. What is important is to live, enjoy what one has, and be glad that others can also enjoy.

Life is short…but such a great blessing that we should not let it pass by without enjoying the sunlight of the day.

I learned so much from Alvetta on our trip home. The sad part is that it took me so long. The good part is that I learned.

Thanks, Alvetta

My mind also flashed back to our last cruise. We did nine in all. Our first and last cruises were with Royal Caribbean International. Alvetta loved cruises especially in the Caribbean. So when I asked her what she wanted to do for our 50th Wedding Anniversary, she decided that we'd get our friends and family together, renew our wedding vows and go on a cruise.

We renewed our wedding vows three times in our marriage--on our 25th, 40th and 50th. Each time was a great celebration. Alvetta wanted the 50th celebration to last a year.

Our anniversary cruise was the best one ever. We left Detroit and flew nonstop to San Juan where we boarded our cruise ship "Serenade of the Seas". Part of our original wedding party, friends and relatives joined us for seven days and nights of perfect weather. St. Thomas, St. Marten, Antigua and St. Lucia were some of our ports of call. We joined our party for most of the day trip, but also kept time for just the two of us.

Looking back now I know that Alvetta's cancer had started. I could not detect anything, but it was there. I also know that Alvetta knew something was wrong.

It did not stop us from enjoying our cruises with family and friends, and all the new-found friends we always attract when we travel. Alvetta had this fit with people and they loved being in her company. So after each trip we would have a new set of friends to contact, send a card to, invite to our house or go to theirs.

Our cruise party was the talk of the ship. 50 years of marriage is a milestone and test of faith. People stopped to wish us luck, how we did it and sent us flowers, wine, candy and other small gifts. It was the very best it could be.

As we boarded the plane for home, someone told the flight crew that we were celebrating our 50 years of marriage. Bottles of champagne came out of nowhere followed by toast after toast. The entire plane became part of our party.

This was in November 2005. It was hard to believe that just four months later, March 2006, Alvetta would be fighting for her life. We would never have believed that just 17 months after our wonderful 50th anniversary celebration, that just a day before her 68th birthday, on June 11, she would leave us.

We've Come This Far by Faith—a song of farewell—stopped my reflections and brought me back to the reality of the present.

As I sang the song of farewell, I knew that the most precious chapter of my life was coming to a close. I knew that I would reflect on this chapter in my life time and time again, and each time I would thank God for all the wondrous years I spent with—

Alvetta

Part II
Sea Shells and a Piece of the Moon

These objects play no part in my life.
I do not live close to the sea,
Nor do I live in outer space.
I cannot touch the sky or reach the stars.
I cannot lose myself in another galaxy.
I cannot feel the still of the night or press the moonbeam to my cheek.
I cannot walk the top of the water;
Nor can I live at the bottom of the sea.
I cannot fly like a bird on mountain high
Or run like a deer against the course of history.
I can not accept things as they should be, but
When I change the "I" to "We", (John & Al)
There is not anything that is impossible for me.

- John C. Moore

The child in me dances
For I have found you.
And the man in me—
Gives thanks.

--John C. Moore

11 Months Thus Far

February 22, 2007

I have missed a lot of days in keeping a daily log. Today, I will start carrying a book with me and recording each day and attempting to recall years and days gone by.

It is hard to believe that almost 11 months have passed since Alvetta had her operation on March 27, 2006. She was given six months to live.

February 21, 2007

Alvetta still looks good. If you walk in for a few minutes you would ask—"Why is she here? But after a few minutes you can sense some of the problem." She lies in bed with shaking hands, repeating the same words, falling asleep, continuing to pull at her blanket, asking to be put on the bedpan over and over.

After each meal she forgets what she ate and laments, "Why didn't they feed me?" She is also sleeping more and talking less.

She is staring out of the window or at the TV. I ask what she is watching and she tells me she doesn't know.

February 22, 2007

I wanted to attend a good friend's funeral service that was to start at 10:00 a.m., so I called Hospice to check on Alvetta as I do every morning.

The nurse told me the doctors wanted to talk to me about Alvetta's condition. I told her of my plans and she said she thought it would be best if I would hurry to Hospice—Alvetta was having serious problems.

When I arrived, Alvetta was truly out of it, not able to talk or focus. The doctor stated that she might have had a seizure, stroke, some swelling of the brain or either a low or high sugar count.

I thought this was it and called Audrey to very quietly call Nana and Gramps to come to Hospice, but not to rush and panic them.

They arrived and Alvetta was still out of it, but later on started to show signs of recovery. The next day she was back but did not recall what happened the previous day.

In my mind I thought, "This is the way it is going to happen." The brain will swell, Alvetta will go into a coma, the tumor will grow and we will lose her.

The rest of the day I felt so alone. Although my grieving started in March of 2006, the thought of Alvetta's passing really hurt deeply.

This was also the date of my appointment to see a pulmonary specialist to check out my lungs. I had to take an x-ray and a breathing test. The results were not that great. I have asbestosis and it seems to be spreading. The doctor thinks I am moving from Level I to Level II. I'm not to worry. Hopefully, modern medicine can keep me from Level III, which is the final level.

I arrived late at Hospice that day. I had asked Nana and Gramps to stay there until I showed up. Alvetta had a room full of company. Our friends Hortense (Tense) Ward and Mattie Rice, our granddaughter Nikki and her son Christian were there among others.

Alvetta looked ok, but her face revealed problems. She asked me to get her an ice cream bar out of the freezer. (We had them at home). She also asked if we could stop by the house on our way. I did not know where we were supposed to go.

I can see a change each day. We lose a little more of her each day. Alvetta does not want to revisit the fact she is dying. So I guess I will not bring it up again.

Her parents are grieving and as well as the rest of the family. The ones I fear for the most are Ric, our son, her mom and dad, and Nikki, our granddaughter.

Today she talked about attending the University of Toledo. I will ask Tense to write a little bit about this time in Alvetta's life.

⇒A Pair of Shoes!⇐

Tense's Story

We met in a Math class at the University of Toledo. We became friends instantly—she liked the shoes I wore!

I invited her to join our study group. Later, we decided our husbands should meet. They met at John's birthday party and hit it off.

My husband, Dorsey and I invited them to spend the weekend with us at our cottage at Fox Lake and that began a wonderful friendship.

We traveled many places together, Al and I, shopping, Delta Sigma Theta sorority conventions, school conventions and Charms, Inc. conventions.

As a foursome, we cruised the Caribbean Islands and toured Italy. In between we were at the lake, playing cards, golfing and shopping. It was a lasting friendship that began with a pair of shoes.

H. Hortense Ward

After 6 p.m.

February 23, 2007

I arrived to find Alvetta smiling and asking, "Where have you been?" I gave her the newspaper with a story of one of our friends whose mother just celebrated her 100th birthday. This is a blessing and a great mystery—why do some of us die young and others go on forever?

The volunteers of Hospice had put in fresh flowers, and water and asked if we wanted to pray, take communion, or just talk. I know the need to talk grows everyday. Not about Alvetta dying, but the rest of us living.

The volunteers are eager to provide support in so many ways, not only to the patients, but also to the families. This really helps to reduce stress. Just talking helps with exhaustion and morale. The world needs more trained volunteers in every step of our lives and Hospice of Northwest Ohio knows how to do it.

Alvetta is having a good day. Marcia—Alvetta's first cousin, Tense and Sister Mary, a Hospice volunteer, have joined her for lunch.

I can hear her thoughts more and more. She is saying over and over, "Don't leave me alone". When I am in the room I know that the help of family and friends is the best medicine that she can have at this point.

It is hard watching when someone you love has a limited time on this earth. Each day you are left with a little less of the person than the day before. It's funny at this time you can actually hear the thoughts of your loved one if you watch and listen with your heart and not your ears.

If you listen with your heart you can have intimate and meaningful conversations. You can relive special moments and the two of you can travel back and forth thorough time and space.

This is the time to say things that need to be said, explain things that need to be explained and to forgive each other for the small things that need forgiveness. You also realize at this time that most things that need forgiveness are so small and how precious life really is. The time now is to enjoy each second you have with each other.

There should be a program for families that take place after 6 p.m. The professionals are on duty from 9 to 5. I have discovered that most of the pain sets in after 6 p.m. If you live alone after having lived with someone for years, that's the time you realize what you are losing and how lonely you will be. That is the time you need help.

February 24, 2007

I arrived at 11:15 a.m. Pinky, one of Alvetta's YMCA friends, was with her. Alvetta seemed to really enjoy her conversation with Pinky. She was looking like everything was ok, but I had this strange feeing that she had slipped a little overnight. Her nurse said that all was ok. Her blood sugar reading was 275. This was now an average morning reading for Alvetta with around 325 at night. 100-120 is normal.

She told Pinky we would be going out for Chinese. She had a taste for General Tso's chicken and egg rolls. She is confused on what time of day it is. She is staring at the TV, not really watching it.

For the last couple of days the weather has been sunny and the snow from a storm we had a week ago is melting. A feeling of spring is in the air. It could be the start of a great new season and an old season starting to disappear. It is hard to believe I have been coming to Hospice everyday for almost 90 days straight.

Each day I fill out Alvetta's menu for the next day. I have had lunch here almost every day. The food is good, but I am tired of eating here. At the end of the day, I head home. It is really wearing on me. The hardest part is returning to an empty house and knowing it will always be like this.

February 25, 2007

The weather predicted did not turn out as bad as they had led us to believe. The ice did come and the roads were bad, but by noon the warm weather had cleared the roads.

When I called Alvetta at 9:30 a.m. she said she was very sleepy. I told her I would be out before she had lunch. Her blood sugar reading was up to 495. She had to have 12 units of insulin. It also may have been the reason for all the confusion. Ric was upset with the questions that did not make sense.

Audrey told Alvetta that her blood sugar numbers were causing her to mix things up, but she did not want to hear it. We were the ones confused. After Ric and Audrey left, she kept asking for the bedpan—false alarms. She also wanted me to help her to the toilet although she has not been able to walk for the last month.

Alvetta has lost interest in her favorite TV shows. She has the TV on, but is not watching or listening to her favorite shows. Whatever channel is on is fine with her. At one time she knew and accepted that she was dying. In the last 45 days she has not wanted to talk about it. So I talked about our past 52 years. This is getting to be hard and full of confusion.

February 26, 2007

Alvetta's blood sugar readings are still high, over 300. Ric came to see her. She was very confused and Ric was upset once more. He stayed for about an hour and then Nana and Gramps came. Alvetta perked up a little. I started to walk around as I do when she has company. This is my way of releasing stress and it helps to pass the time of day. As her mom and dad were leaving, Sally, a long time friend, walked in and I went for another walk. I visited other patients and staff. I noticed a familiar face and then it hit me that this was the Kenneth Marney family. Kenneth passed away months ago. I heard a cry and went to see what was wrong. Kenneth's brother, Eugene has just passed away. He was four doors down from Alvetta and had been there only for a couple of days. He was dead and the family was gathering.

It struck me that in a little while we would repeat this scene with Alvetta. I asked the staff to watch over her as I prepared to go home and left my telephone number. I thought the next 24 hours would be hard on Alvetta if she continues to act in the same manner.

I can tell the cancer is spreading.

February 27, 2007

I left home at 11:30 a.m. heading for Hospice, not knowing what to expect. Yesterday she was very confused and her face had started to swell once more. The Hospice staff was giving her the best of care, but

I still felt guilty. Had I allowed her to be put in Hospice too soon? It's almost three months now. At home in the middle of the night I wake up asking myself that question again and again and again.

As I walked into Hospice, I knew that I had done the right thing. The place where she is residing, the location, the quality of staff and their understanding of the dying experience cannot be duplicated.

On this day she was showing more signs. She was asleep when I walked into the room. Her face did not look good. She was very warm to the touch. Her face was flushed as if she had on makeup. I sat down very quietly so as not to awaken her. Her breathing pattern was changing and decreasing. She did not look relaxed in this sleep stage. She was holding very tightly on the bed rails as if we thought she was falling and had to hold on to save herself.

The tears started to fall and I couldn't stop them so I went into the bathroom to wash my face so that Alvetta could not see my tears.

After examining her, the doctor explained that Alvetta was losing the battle. The confusing questions Alvetta asked us all were an indication of approaching death. He asked her why she was at Hospice. She said, "Because John was worn out." She did not mention cancer.

I asked the doctor to have a talk with Alvetta's parents as soon as possible. They think she is getting better.

February 28, 2007

I didn't sleep last night. My thoughts were on Alvetta's condition yesterday. Each time I think I am prepared for the worse, something lets me know that I am not. The weight of the last 12 months is starting to show. Last night or early morning, I went back to bed. Like I stated earlier, I could not sleep. I tossed and turned. I got up, walked the floors, watched a little TV and then went back to bed. This time I felt Alvetta's presence. It was as if she walked into the room, had very lightly gotten into bed and rolled over to my side. I could really feel her warm body next to mine. We embraced and the next thing I knew it was 7 a.m. and she was gone. It was as if she had slept in the bed all night with me. I got up refreshed for the first time in months.

⇛Explanations and Challenges⇚

Back at Hospice, Ric, Kyla, Nana and Gramps all showed up as well as a couple of people from church. Alvetta is very confused. The nurses are worried about her. Her sugar readings are all over 300 now. She is confused night and day. I want the doctors to sit down with Nana and Gramps to explain Alvetta's condition.

March 1, 2007

Alvetta's blood sugar is a big concern. They may do some changes in her diet. She keeps asking for things she shouldn't have. They have increased her Metformin, a diabetes medicine, to 2000 mg. per day. She is still asking about people who may have been here a week ago as if they are in the other room.

The last few months have proven to me that Hospice of Northwest Ohio is designed to provide the best end of life service for Alvetta and all of us who love her. I know there are times I feel very guilty about having put her here, but as I arrive every day I know it is the right thing. She needs around the clock care and professionals to provide it.

I have asked the doctor to meet with Alvetta's parents on Friday to talk about what is happening and what to expect.

The time we talk now is very limited. I cannot talk about plans for the funeral and what she wants to give away. She does not want to talk about Glioblastoma, the chemotherapy, radiation or the surgery. It is as if they never happened. Even when the doctor asked her why she was at Hospice, the answer was, "Because John was worn out." This is perhaps her way of protecting herself.

March 2, 2007

The doctors will meet with Alvetta's parents today. They will be told that the steroids will keep the brain pressure from increasing too fast, but cannot stop it. The steroids also make her too weak to walk. This will help them better understand that for a small time period, Alvetta may look like she is improving to loved ones, but she is not and will not.

The Hospice medical staff is doing all it can to boost her immune functions, reduce swelling and inflammation. They are doing all they can to suppress tumor growth.

Each day I can tell that I am losing my partner of 51 years. I do not need the doctors to tell me. I say my prayers for Alvetta each day. At first they were for her to get better. Now it's "Please go". "Alvetta would not want a life of just laying in the bed. Let her come home to You."

March 3, 2007

It's very windy sunny day. Another Saturday. More than that, it marks three months since Alvetta was taken to Hospice. At the time she left home, I thought it would only be a few weeks, not months.

Things have changed. Alvetta shows signs of weakness and confusion. She is not asking to go home and is talking only a short time to the visitors and me.

I call her every morning at 9:00 a.m. Her voice is getting weaker. She always asks, "Why are you not here?" I tell her what time it is and that I will be there in an hour.

Each day she receives more cards, flowers and visitors. Two of our oldest friends, Grace and Chuck, who lived next door to us over 25 years ago just found out about her condition and came by to see Alvetta.

Tim, Pinky, Ric, Sister Mary and a few others stopped by.

I really feel better about Alvetta's' parents meeting with the Hospice doctor. She did an excellent job of explaining Alvetta's Glioblastoma Multiforme, and that it is a Grade 4, which is deadly. They now know the brain tumor is growing slowly. Alvetta is in no pain. As the growth continues, so will her confusion. All is being done to keep her comfortable. We cannot tell how long she will live. We do know she will not recover.

We pray for mercy.

March 4, 2007

Alvetta's sugar count is still high. She still wants to eat. We have to be careful not to give her fruit and sugar-laden foods.

When I arrive, Audrey and Sandra, another of Alvetta's cousins, are in the room. The nurses had taken Alvetta down for a bath. So I go down the hall to meet them. Alvetta is being rolled back to the room. She is smiling, looking cleaned, refreshed and very relaxed. She calls out when she sees me "There's my man." The nurses get a big kick out of that.

After everyone was gone, I could tell the trip and bath were tiring to her. She went right off to sleep and slept most of the day. She is not talking much. She listens and stares at the TV, window, or ceiling. Her movements are slow. Her long-term memory is excellent but short-term memory decreases daily. She does not talk about going home or trips to the stores or casinos, or even driving to Florida. Each day she asks if I have talked to the kids and how long I planned to stay.

This is hard on everyone as we watch her leaving us. We know that her time is near, but we do not want to give her up. Yes, God knows best, but do I have to agree?

March 5, 2007

One of the Hospice volunteers said she works at Hospice because the people who are dying are close to God and she can feel His presence. Alvetta's face is a good indication of what she means. Her face is aglow. She is not using makeup but she looks as if a makeup artist arrives everyday to brush her cheeks, apply lipstick and put a sparkle in her eyes. God must have assigned a special angel for Alvetta to create this special effect.

Everyone who walks into the room remarks on how beautiful she looks. She then smiles, and the room is aglow.

I am glad I have a sign posted that lets visitors know not to bring food. Her sugar readings are very high. Fruit, sweets and snack food will only increase it. People mean well and always want to feed the sick. Hospice has a great menu and also healthy snacks. It does the patient no good to have someone bring fried foods, fast foods, etc., without knowing the person's condition.

Alvetta not only has cancer, she has high blood pressure, diabetes and is very overweight. So, we have to be careful.

March 6 & 7, 2007

Alvetta had a lot of company on the 6th and 7th. Neither were good days for her. Kyla, Shanon, Tim, Nana, Gramps, Ric and more visited and had a good time. Alvetta spent the rest of the time sleeping after company left on both days.

She appears to be more attentive than other days, but it lasts for an hour or two. She is in no pain. She still has a great attitude and still loves her meals. I need to talk to the doctors. On the 10th of March she will have been in Hospice for 100 days.

I think she is wasting away. Not in size. In fact, she has gained weight because of her appetite and inactivity. Each day I watch a little of her mental powers diminish. Nothing seems important except the next meal. She will talk, but only for a few minutes. The quality of life is diminishing in my eyesight. Others may not be able to see it.

I know that the angels of Hospice are doing all they can do to make her comfortable. Maybe it is me. I am so tired that I might not be at the right mind to judge her condition.

March 8, 2007

I called Alvetta at 9:15 a.m. as I do each day. She seemed to be in good spirits and was wondering why I was not there yet. I could tell by the tone of her voice that this was going to be a good day.

When I arrived, she was awake, smiling and asking, "Where have you been?" I combed and brushed her hair like I have been doing everyday on my arrival. Also, like I do everyday, I removed all the papers and books and got the room ready for her daily visitors. This was the day that I gave each of the shifts signed copies of my book on stress. It was the talk of the morning and afternoon shifts.

Alvetta was up talking to her guests and kidding with the nurses and aides. She asked me to call her mother. She asked about the grandkids. Then she wanted to know if we were packed to go to Florida.

You Are My Life

March 9, 2007

I arrived at Hospice early. I wanted to talk to the doctors. Alvetta is just lying in the bed. I wanted her to sit in a chair. I wanted to be able to turn the bed around so she could look out the window and see the outside. I also thought that if we could get her in a chair we could roll her around outside of her room.

The doctor examined Alvetta and felt that although there didn't appear to be much growth from the cancer, it did appear that there was more damage from the steroids. The steroids are given to control swelling of the brain.

Alvetta has been on steroids for a long time and I am afraid they are producing both physical and mental problems. The swelling of her face, hands and legs are more noticeable. There is a potential for softening of the bones. I know she is weaker and her diabetes is almost out of control.

The doctors will meet on March 12 to discuss what to do. Perhaps they will reduce the steroids. They tried this once before and Alvetta had a mild seizure. The doctors also talked about having another MRI done to determine the growth of the tumor. This would mean moving her to a hospital for the test. This could be very dangerous in her current condition.

March 10, 2007

We had lots of company but Alvetta slept all day. I knew this was going to happen. After a couple of good days she slips. Saturdays and Sundays are good days for visitors. The temperature was close to 50. The snow is just about gone. The smell of spring is in the air.

I had arrived at my usual time. Alvetta was asleep, so I did my little cleaning up and wait for her to awaken. When she did, she wanted to know what was for breakfast. I told her that it was time for lunch. This is our normal routine.

While she was awake we talked a little about our various trips to Canada, mostly the ones to Toronto. On one occasion we went by bus with a large group and partied all weekend. We caught the nightspots, the tourist attractions and walked though the popular Underground Railroad for dinner. We shopped all day and danced all night. The old couple with the tour party often asked us when we slept. We would always answer "at home".

Ric showed up at 4:20 p.m. with a large box of cooked crab. I took them to the kitchen and asked them to put them with her meal—minus a few things. They did and Alvetta really enjoyed her special dinner.

She acts ok, but I think she is in a world of her own. She only shows a real interest in her meals. It appears that nothing else matters.

March 11, 2007

It is a beautiful day and the sun is shining. The snow is almost gone. It was also time to "spring the clock forward", so I had to adjust to getting up an hour earlier. I started to read more about Alvetta's condition. I felt it would help me be better prepared if and when I talk with the doctors in the next couple of days.

I think the steroids are creating more problems for Alvetta. I read about the good and bad effects of taking steroids. I don't want her steroids stopped, simply reduced. I know steroids are used to reduce swelling in Alvetta's brain, but I also noticed the weight gain, muscle weakness, mood swings and increased blood sugar levels that are side effects of such treatments.

Sunday was a very good day for Alvetta. She slept from 12:45 p.m. that afternoon to 4:15 p.m. when her parents arrived. After they left, we talked a little but about our first trip to Fordyce, Arkansas with Cathy and Ric in my mother's 1956 Desoto. She laughed about the outhouses, lack of indoor plumbing and life way out in the country. She also reflected on how much the children enjoyed the farm and the animals.

By this time dinner had arrived and I made my plans to leave. She asked me to stay longer and I did. A little later she had forgotten I was in the room. She looked tired. I left like always, not knowing what the next day would bring. I know I am losing her.

March 12, 2007

Alvetta has been in Hospice of Northwest Ohio for 100 days. She entered on December 3. It has been a year since I have known something was wrong. She had the operation on March 27 and on the 30th they told me she had six months at best.

The doctor and I talked in Alvetta's room. The doctor noticed the increased shaking of her hands and the blank stares and thought these could be mini seizures. It was time, she said, to cut down very slowly on the steroids and start seizure medication.

I reflected on what I had read recently about this deadly form of brain cancer.

> *For those over 60, the survival rate for Glioblastoma Multiforme victims is about 3%. The 5-year survival rate has remained unchanged over the past 30 years and stands at less than 3%. Even with all the modern technologies, radiation, surgery, chemotherapy and steroids the survival rate for GMB (Glioblastoma Multiforme) remains very low.*

I don't know much about the treatments. All I know is that I am losing my wife of 51 years. I am tired. I am angry. I am helpless. I have prayed for Alvetta over 365 days. But I am not the only one. Hundreds of others have also prayed for her.

People say, "God knows best" and "Let His will be done." There are times when one really wants to ask Him "Why?" This is my time to ask Him "Why?"

Patent Shoes and Cucumber Sandwiches

Brittney's Story

John and Alvetta (Poppy & Grammy) are my grandparents. My father is Howard "Ric" Moore. Although my sister Malayna and I didn't see them very often growing up because we lived on the West Coast, some of our favorite memories of Grammy are from our childhood visits during the summer.

Grammy loved to dress us up in cute Mary Jane type patent leather shoes with frilly socks. As soon as we arrived in Toledo, we'd go on these wonderful shopping trips and buy new clothes and shoes. I would always try hard not to scuff my new shoes, but then I'd get excited about something and scuff them anyway.

When I first learned how to write, Grammy and I would spend the morning with together as she showed me how to hold my pencils properly and write my alphabets correctly. She may have been on summer vacation from teaching, but she was first and always a teacher!

Grammy and Poppy also loved to host barbeques and parties for friends and family when Malayna and I visited. There'd always be a lot of food and laughter and people that we would try to remember so that we'd know them on our next trip to Toledo.

I remember when we [Malayna, Grammy, and me] planned our first tea party and we invited friends. We picked out beautiful cookies and treats, and Grammy made delicious cucumber sandwiches. We got to dress up and bring out the "good" china and dragon tea service that my Dad had brought from overseas. We hosted tea parties a few years and each time they got bigger and fancier. For a long time it seemed that that dragon tea set would sit in Grammy's china cabinet just for Malayna and me to return and eat dainty cucumber sandwiches on beautiful plates while wearing our patent leather shoes.

Brittney Moore

Your Are My Life

March 13, 2007

Alvetta, as always, was glad to see me and it feels good that she still knows who I am. I have a feeling that someday very soon she will not be able to do so.

There is concern over the mini seizures. I am not concerned, because it is part of the transition. The edema or the tumor is increasing and it helps me prepare for the final outcome.

Her staff of angels has given her even more attention. They respond to her every need. God truly did put angels on Earth and a lot of them are at Hospice of Northwest Ohio.

Today we talked about our last cruise to celebrate our 50th Anniversary. It was one of our best trips. It was hard to believe how much our lives have changed since that happy time less than a year and a half ago.

Alvetta had many visitors today. Nana and Gramps, Shanon and Kyla, Sandra, Tense and others. They, too, have started to notice the increased confusion. They stay later to be with her longer. I left Shanon and Kyla with her. Shanon called me later to tell me that I had not filled out the day's menu. I called in and talked to Kathie, the nurse's aide and told her what to put on Alvetta's menu. I told her that in 101 days this was the first time I had forgotten to fill out the menu. I could hear the tears in her voice as she said. "We love you, John." It really meant a lot to me. They knew and I knew that I was really doing all I could to take care of Alvetta.

You are my life, can't you see.
I can do so much if you are with me.
You are everything I hoped for
Smart, loving, and so much more…
You give new meaning to my life
I thank God for you, my wife.

JCM
January 22, 1983

Reinventing Myself Daily

March 14, 2007

You start to really understand the need to talk to others as you cope with the rapid changes in your partner. The stress is enormous. I am so concerned for myself, but also for all of our family and friends.

Almost each day someone new has called who just found out about Alvetta and asks how she is doing. I try to explain in as little detail as possible about her condition and what Glioblastoma really is. They tell me how many people they know who has had a brain tumor and survived. I try to explain again about Glioblastoma. They mean well. Many offer to mail me information on various cancer cures.

Alvetta's 102nd day at Hospice is full of confusion, seizures and weight gain. Her sugar readings are extremely high ranging between 482-500. She had forgotten that she ate breakfast and lunch. She thinks she is at home and wants me to get food from the cabinets for her.

Nana and Gramps stopped by and witnessed the confusion. Audrey and Jill, a Red Hat club member and friend, spend the lunch hour. After lunch, Alvetta slept until almost 4 p.m.

I find myself at the end of the day with mood swings, shock, depression, anger, guilt, pain, nervousness and lack of sleep. I have to think about the great yesterdays in order to deal with the realities of today.

I know that for me, watching a loved one die has an effect on one's spirituality. I am now asking God to call Alvetta home.

March 15, 2007

Spring was here for a moment. The snow is back. Alvetta was asleep when I arrive at Hospice. I sit next to her. Although I have known for almost a year that this cancer will kill her, I still look at her in disbelief at what is going on inside her brain. The tears start to flow. I feel all of the emotions at one time. Sadness, anger, numbness, helplessness (which is the worse for me), guilt and the rawness of being alone.

Alvetta woke. I had washed my face and reinvented myself for rest of my day with her. Reinventing myself has saved me.

She looked beautiful. Her face looks as if she has put on fresh makeup. The steroids, along with making her face fat, also gives it a glow. We talked about her morning. Who were her nurse and nurse's aide for the day? Who picked out the gown she had on? How was breakfast? Did she have company? Who brought the fresh flowers? She did not know the answers to any of the questions of the present. So I turned to the past.

She talked about Saint Benedict's Catholic Church, the classes and masses that she attended. She asked me why they tore down her church and beloved school. She talked about her classmates. She talked about Sister Mary Yvonne, whom she loved so much that she adopted the name Yvonne as her middle name.

We were married there on November 5, 1955. The church and school were torn down in 1965.

March 16, 2007

This was not a good day. From the time I arrived at 11:00 a.m. I knew this was not going to be a good day. She did not look like she did on most days. Her voice was a little shaky and weak. She gave me a little smile but did not ask questions.

The day before the nurse had given me a journal to keep up with the mini seizures. After a good lunch, Alvetta went to sleep for three hours. Her breathing was very shallow and she appeared to be fighting with someone in her sleep.

The first seizure occurred at 3:10 p.m. and lasted for about 5 seconds. I sat and watched then it was gone. The next one was 10 minutes later for about 10 seconds. The 3:20 p.m. seizure occurred at the change of the morning and afternoon shifts and lasted for a few minutes. I rushed out to tell the staff, but the changing shift created confusion so the doctor and her assistant came down to check. They examined Alvetta and thought maybe more fluid had caused some problems around the brain.

Alvetta did not recall having any problems. She asked to be propped up in bed. The nurses told her she was up as high as she could go. They rearranged her for comfort as she complained about pain in her back. However, the nurses felt it must be the growing tumor causing her to be so confused. They will keep a close eye on her tonight.

March 17, 2007

Each time I walk into Hospice it is with mixed emotions. First I am greeted by name by the staff on duty. They say "Good morning" and "Hi" "Nice Day" "How was your evening?" They greet me with smiles and lower my concerns for a few moments. Then I enter my partner's room and I know the reality of Glioblastoma. The pace slows every day. Her bed is now her prison. It is very difficult for me wanting to do so much for her and knowing that I can now do nothing.

Now we just sit. She wants me close by. We hold hands. We talk. I do most of the talking. I ask her questions about the past. I ask her about her stay in Brand Whitlock. I ask her address there—320. I ask who lived next door---Casey Jones' mother. This is how we talk.

She still smiles. She has a great sense of humor. She is very comfortable but she is still living with a brain tumor and has been at Hospice now for 105 days.

The staff loves her. Even the ones who have been reassigned to other rooms still come in to talk with her. I know the family will go through a lot of pain when Alvetta passes. But I also know that the staff will not only feel our pain, but will have pain of their own.

Reinventing myself each day is hard, very hard.

March 18, 2007

Alvetta was asleep when I arrived on Sunday. I talked to the nurses. She had her bath and had on one of her red nightgowns. She looked at peace. The nurse said her sugar level was good that morning at 165. Audrey had arrived before me and said that Alvetta had not been talking all morning. Audrey wondered if Alvetta was still having seizures and if they had adjusted her medication levels. I told her that they had made a few adjustments and would monitor her behavior closely.

At noon they served her lunch. She was ready to eat. She tried to hold her soup, bread and fork in her hand while she ate. She has done this more lately. She has spilled food time and time again on herself. I have to make certain that they put her hot coffee in a safe container so that she does not hurt herself.

Each day gets harder and harder to sit, so I walk the halls upstairs and downstairs, talk to a few people. But mostly I sit from 11:30 a.m. to 6:00 p.m. each day. And each day she gets a little weaker, more confused, and is losing some movement.

I KNOW I NEED TO SEE A DOCTOR BUT I MUST HOLD OFF UNTIL Alvetta's last days. I want everyone's attention on her. She is a fighter and a very positive role model for us all.

March 19, 2007

Alvetta has been in Hospice of Northwest Ohio for 107 days. Most people think Hospice takes patients with only a few days left to live, but the handbook of Hospice of Northwest Ohio. states: *Patients are encouraged to seek assistance from Hospice when it is believed they have a life expectancy of six months or less. Our patients often tell us: We wish we'd entered your Hospice program sooner."*

Today as I walked into Alvetta's room, I was a little afraid. She just didn't look right. I went looking for her nurse and ran into her doctor. The doctor said she had given Alvetta medication to slow down the sudden seizure attacks. The medication would hopefully stop the seizures, but would leave Alvetta in a more relaxed, laid back state, and even sleeping more than before.

She had company early, but kept asking when the little girl was going to show up, meaning Kyla, our granddaughter. Ric arrived at about 3:45 p.m. and then Shanon and Kyla. Alvetta smiled in a very relaxed way but I could tell her day was made. Shanon cut her hair. She made small talk with Ric and really laughed as Kyla went into her two year old things that 2-year-olds do.

They left at 5. Her dinner arrived and I helped her to eat. She was very tired when I left. This was still a good day for Alvetta.

Call Us Mom and Dad

Shanon's Story

I vividly remember the first time I met Ric's mom in person and how I felt. The meeting was not a set up introduction as Ric and I had known each other for only a few months and had only been on a couple of dates. It just so happened that I was picking Ric up at his parents' home where he lived for a short time after getting out of the Navy. I had arrived at the house to pick him up and he was not ready to leave. He wanted me to meet his mother who was in the other room. So, of course, I gave him the "Look"--the kind of look everyone gives when being unexpectedly introduced to any of "The Parents."

He walked with me to the other room and politely introduced me to his mother as his friend, Shanon. I said, "Hello, it's nice to meet you", and then turned around to look at Ric and he was gone.

Mrs. Moore was sitting at a table in their living room, grading her students' papers when we walked in. So I just stood there and smiled. She asked me to have a seat and went back to her students' papers. I sat across from her in silence. She then peered over her glasses at me with "the teacher look" and said, "So how old are you anyway?" Instantly I felt as though I had shrunk a few inches and was back in 5th grade, getting called on by the teacher when I didn't know the answer. I replied that I was 21. She asked about my work and engaged in small talk until Ric finally appeared. We exchanged the usual "nice to have met yous" and I was ready to leave from what felt like being held after class by the teacher.

From then on, as I became more acquainted with the family, I really didn't know how I was supposed to address the "Parents." Being a teacher, a woman, and a mom, she finally said to me one day, "You may call us Mom and Dad." So from then on, Mom and Dad it was. As time went on, we celebrated holidays, birthdays, as well as casual dinners and conversations.

They've been with us through every important event in our lives: engagement, marriage (wondering if it would ever happen, I think), home buying, the struggle to start our family, the pure joy at finally having Kyla and being there for her birth. Yes, John and Alvetta Moore have truly become my Mom and Dad.

I wish Mom was still with us to help lead and teach Kyla to be the best woman and person she can be, but hopefully I learned enough from Mom to pass her knowledge along. I miss Mom, and Kyla will miss her more than she'll ever know.

Shanon M. Moore

Memories Keep Me Going

March 21, 2007

I don't know if it is the new medication or the growth of the tumor, but it is wearing on Alvetta. For the first time, she did not eat all of her breakfast and only a small amount of lunch. I left Diane to help her finish dinner. Diane recalled, "She did not want to eat and I made her mad trying to get her to do so." She just wanted to sleep and not talk to anyone.

This was the time I really needed someone to talk to. I was looking for answers or reassurance from someone to reinforce that I was doing all the right things. A sympathetic ear. Someone to ask the right questions.

At home it was the same empty house. It was if all of the air had been pulled out of the house. I could not breathe, I could not eat. And, I could not sleep.

I know what I should be doing now. All of the professional state "take care of yourself", "take time for yourself", "discuss your feelings", "get support and talk to clergy". I should be reaching out for support.

One of these days the professionals will have to understand that some people may never ask for help, but still need it. If they cannot figure this out why should we call them "professionals"! My frustration is beginning to show.

Lend Me Your Ear!

Professionals around, lend an ear!
Where are you when I need you here?
I may not be able to ask in your way,
But my wife is dying! What can you say?
I cannot breathe. I cannot sleep.
I will not, cannot continue to weep!
Can not you see the pain in my face?
As I wander 'round this lonely place?
What have I done wrong? What can I do?
I don't know what to ask? Do you?!

JCM

March 22, 2007

I did not know what to expect today. I left last night with a feeling that I would be called to return to Hospice. The call never came so now I am back. Alvetta is fast asleep, looking very tired. Our day is one of worry and deep concern. I know now the time is near. A few days—maybe a few weeks--but not much more.

My pain has increased because we are not talking. She sleeps and my mind wanders back to happier times. I go over the good and bad times. The birth of the children—meeting Audrey and the boys. All of the trips we had together. Audrey and Alvetta becoming truly mother and daughter. Malayna and Brittney spending the summers with us. Taking Audrey and the boys to the Smokies. Ric returning from the Navy. Nicole and Cory becoming important parts of our lives.

These are the memories that keep me going. They help me to reinvent myself each day. My faith gives me the power to wake up each day and get ready for what ever the day will bring.

March 23, 2007

Each day I see Hospice of Northwest Ohio living up to its vision. "To provide care and education that positively transforms the way people view and experience the end of life." I watch the staff show compassion for the patients and the families. The teamwork.

If government and big business could work like this, what a better country we would have. I am so impressed with the dignity and respect shown to each of us regardless of color, creed or mental level. Its days like this that the guilty feeling of taking Alvetta to Hospice is at its lowest.

While I arrived she was awake and waiting. We talked about five minutes. She slept for an hour until lunch arrived. I also picked up lunch and we ate together. She ate very slowly and talked only if she was asked a question. I could see it was work to feed herself, but she did not want me to do it. After dinner she fell asleep and woke up when Sister Mary asked if we wanted communion. We did.

One of the nurses stopped by to check in. She was ready to change shifts. She would be off until Monday and wanted Alvetta to know.

At this point visitors started to arrive. Aunts, uncles, parents, grandkids, great-grandkids and friends. They stayed only a little while. She was glad to see them all. She fell asleep the minute they left and I had to wake her up for dinner.

March 24, 2007

I phone at my regular time to talk to Alvetta. She always waits for my call after breakfast. She does not answer. I call back and ask one of the nurses to check on her. I told the nurse to let her know I had called and would be out at the regular time.

My next routine each morning is to call family and a few friends to give them an update on Alvetta's condition. I really do not like this part and tell them the same story over and over, but I feel it is very important. They love her and are very concerned about me. So, I make the calls.

Alvetta is eating well, but not as much. She is not asking for extra food. She is also eating very slowly. She is now sleeping more. These are very deep sleeps. In the past I could wake her up by just moving in the room. Now it doesn't bother her. Now she awakes confused and not really wanting to talk.

One of her favorite uncles arrived from New York to see her. In the past she would have been very excited. He talked about the great times he and his family had at our home. Alvetta just looked and smiled. He was glad that he came to see her and knows she is dying. This was his goodbye to her.

March 25, 2007

The sky is bright, and the day is warm. I arrive early to make certain that if Alvetta had company they would not stay too long. I could tell that she is not in the mood to entertain. I think some people who go to visit hospitals go only to find out the latest scoop. They should be there for comfort and respect for the family. The fact that Alvetta is in Hospice means that she is dying.

The questions are asked over and over again about the type of cancer, whether she will go home, why she is here, how much this is costing us, whether we got a second, third or even fourth opinion. The questions go on and on.

I am really looking for quiet time. I hope that someone will write a manual on what to ask and what to say to families and the patient in times like this. All we want is for someone to pray. Someone to hold her hand. Someone to give her communion. A hug, a card, and most of all, a smile.

Alvetta is my hero. She takes it all in with a smile on her face. She never complains to friends, family or staff. She tells me in a few minutes time as we talk about her pain, concerns and needs. Her faith gets stronger every day. She is a fighter. She has been at it now for almost a year. As I look at her, the problems of the world become smaller and so are the people who are always complaining.

March 26, 2007

Hattchie, one of Alvetta's oldest friends from Dayton with whom she spent her teenage summers, called and told me she was on a bus and had just arrived in Findlay, about an hour away. We told her that someone would pick her up at the bus station. Hattchie is a whole book by herself. To know her is to love her. She would do anything for Alvetta.

The thought that Hattchie would be coming to Hospice made Alvetta's day. The room was full of visitors when she showed up. At once the room became Hattchie's. Alvetta and Hattchie talked, whispered, laughed and joked. Alvetta mostly listened as Hattchie relived their times in Dayton. These were times that were only revealed in whispers. Secrets that only they could share.

True friends have a certain magic that people who have never had true friends can only imagine, but will never understand. It is almost like a bond made in heaven. It may be stronger than marriage, because most truly good friends last a lifetime.

Hattchie knows her good friend is dying. She does not come to ask questions. She came to love, share and relieve. Alvetta smiled, laughed and for a little while, I could see the teenager again reborn.

We all laughed and enjoyed the moment. I know that tomorrow would be a hard day for Alvetta, but on this day, thanks to Hattchie, it was wonderful.

March 27, 2007

A year ago today, Alvetta had her operation. It was also at this time that I was told she had six months to live. I did not share this with her parents. Their faith is strong and there should always be hope.

I knew when I arrived at Hospice that Alvetta would be tired. She was asleep. I rearranged her room like I have done for the past 114 days. I put fresh water in the containers holding fresh-cut flowers and into the flowerpots. I put up her cards for the day and tossed yesterday's paper, putting the new one out. Each day I bring in the newspaper. In the beginning, she would read a little, but now she is not reading at all. I still bring it.

I had to wake Alvetta up when lunch arrived. The Hospice staff is taking extra care with her meals. They not only serve them, it is the way they do it that lets me know they care. They bring the highest level of knowledge and skill in everything they do.

I had to feed her and she ate only half the food. The nurse came in and asked her if she wanted something else. She said no. When the nurse left, I cried. The tears just poured down. I could not stop. Alvetta, thank God, had fallen asleep. I knew yesterday this wouldn't be a good day for her. I also know that a bad day for her is now a really awful day for me.

March 28, 2007

Alvetta did not answer the telephone this morning. I didn't ask the nurse to check on her. I knew she was asleep and left home earlier than usual to check on her. I did not know what to expect. The nurse said she had a rough night, but did not want any medication. They had given her a bath and a massage. This helps her to relax and sleep. I sat and read a book by James Patterson—***Cross***. I am now reading more and watching less TV. This is the best way for me to spend the day. It is the best new way for me to cope while my wife is dying.

This was the first day in 116 days that Alvetta did not have company. I was glad because I wanted her to myself. Just the two of us in a quiet room. Although she was not talking and slept most of the time, we could still communicate in ways that two people do who have been married for over 50 years.

She woke up to a lunch of roast beef, carrots, mashed potatoes, soup and rice pudding. I cut up her meat and fed her. She consumed a third of her lunch. After she had had enough and wanted to sleep, she grabbed my hand and would not let go. I sat down, lowered her bed and did not let her hand go until she was fast asleep.

I cried as I tried to imagine my life without her and the anticipation of the ongoing grief I'd bear.

Thirsty
I was born thirsty
I drank of Fun
    Silence
        Knowledge
           Despair
                I drank of your love's fullness.
                I thirst no more.

                          JCM, 1978

⇁Alvetta is Smiling Today, Lord⇀

March 29, 2007

Each night I ask God to give me the energy for one more day. I pray for a good night's sleep so I can face another day of walking into Alvetta's room with a smile on my face. The wonderful staff at Hospice is helping me to prepare for the death of my wife. They talk to me more, hug me more, stop in the room more to see how we are doing and ask me if I am taking care of myself.

Alvetta is asleep this day as I step in very quietly so as not to wake her. I watch her breathing. They rhythm seems to be off. It is not as deep as I imagined it to be only a few days ago.

I can remember when she was sick once before in the 70s. We lived on Lincoln Avenue. The kids were very young. We were in Omaha, Nebraska and Alvetta got was sick in the back of the car. The kids and I sat in the front seat and drove the many miles home to get her help. She was sick for almost a week. A new doctor in town, Dr. Rowan, came to the house to take care of her. I thought that was an awful time, but that was mild compared to now.

She awoke for lunch but did not feel like eating. I got her to eat her soup. She did not want any of the other food including her dessert. Before, she would sometimes want dessert first.

I tried to create a meaningful discussion with her but she was not up to it.

March 30, 2007

Alvetta is smiling today as I arrive. She asks me, "Where have you been?" She asks about her lunch, the children, her parents and the weather. After I answer her questions, she falls asleep and remains that way until lunch arrives. I start reading another book.

Like yesterday, she ate only a little of her lunch with my help. She looked around after lunch confused about what time of day it is. I tried again to talk to her about how she was feeling, if she knew what was happening to her, if she wanted to put anything aside for the children or grandchildren. She did not want to talk. So I just sat next to her and held her hand until she fell asleep.

I walked the halls of Hospice looking for answers to questions I did now know how to form. How do you to talk to a loved one who is dying? I want us to have this moment. I feel worthless, helpless and frightened. All my life I have been upbeat with a positive attitude, but for over a year I have been dealing with a loved one's dying and my world has changed.

Alvetta is awake and says she is hungry. She needed help to eat dinner. She smiled and told me she was having a good dinner. Sam the dog walks in and she called his name. It is hard to understand after her actions of the last few days.

Dorothy, Alvetta & Sam

Dorothy' Story

Alvetta visited my house with my sister-in-law Gertrude Randall one day after they finished work. The following year I was hired at the same place. Alvetta and I hit it off at the start. This was 1965. We have been friends ever since. We didn't travel together very often, but when needed, we were always there for each other. I reminded her that we sometimes didn't talk for nearly a year, but when we called each other it was just like yesterday. She agreed.

The first project that we worked on as friends was papering my bathroom. After that, we went to her house and papered one of hers. Alvetta moved more than once, and she called me to help a couple of times. She would always ask me to move near her whenever she moved. I said, "No way, Alvetta. As soon as I move, you will find another house and leave me." I'm still in my first house after over 47 years.

We had lots of fun. While at the Welfare Department, we decided that we would stay married to the same person and celebrate our 50th anniversaries. We made it. The only difference was that my husband doesn't like the water so we didn't go on the 50th anniversary cruise with Alvetta and John. I did go over and look at all the pictures.

Before having brain surgery in March 2006, I reminded her of what she told me years ago when we worked together at the Lucas County Welfare department. She was always a good listener to my problems. She would say, "This too shall pass." I repeated that to her. She said, "I hope so."

She survived the surgery. In December of that year Alvetta was taken to Hospice because of falling often. John couldn't handle picking her up. I understood, having the same problem with my aunt.

I visited Alvetta for lunch one day with a very nice person, our friend, Hortense. I didn't visit very much after that because of the resident dog named "Sam". Alvetta asked me why I didn't come by myself to visit. I told her that she just didn't know. She said, "I know". And she did. Alvetta knew about my lifelong fear of large animals, and Sam was a large dog. I knew that Sam was gentle and would probably be asleep if I went to Hospice by myself, but I just couldn't bring myself to try.

Alvetta agreed to talk on the phone when I wanted to visit. I told her that if she wanted me to, that I would come over to see her, "Sam and all". She said "Sam and all"? I said yes.

About two weeks later, I had a dream that she had called me. I woke up knowing that she could no longer make phone calls, so I called Hospice. Audrey, her stepdaughter, answered the phone and asked if I wanted to speak to Alvetta. I said that I would like to talk to her in person. I told Audrey about the dream and wanted to come and see Alvetta. I asked Audrey if she would meet me at the elevator, and she said that she would.

We didn't talk much, but it was nice seeing Alvetta. I needed to know that she was doing ok. I told her that I missed her e-mails. She smiled.

On Saturday, June 9, 2007, I remembered that the following Tuesday would be Alvetta's birthday. I called to have a small cake delivered to her from a bakery, but the bakery said that they did not deliver. After I hung up the phone, I called Hospice to see how she and John were doing. John answered the phone and said that they thought they would lose Alvetta the night before because of the seizures. He had been there all night.

Alvetta and I used to get together and have lunch on our birthdays and split the bill. Mine is in August. Last year, in June 2006, because of her illness, Alvetta invited her closest friends to her house a few days before her birthday for a pajama party. This was my first ever PJ party and here I was --70. With Alvetta, I experienced many "firsts". If it hadn't been for her, I wouldn't have done a lot of things.

One thing that I always said about Alvetta was "Alvetta thinks that all her friends should be friends with each other." Through her, I've made many new friends.

Dorothy Randall

The Flickering Flame

March 31, 2007

The weather is cold and rain is falling. Alvetta is not answering my phone call. I am home cleaning the house and suddenly wonder—why am I cleaning? I will come home to an empty house. So, I put on my coat and head out for another day at Hospice.

I do not have the will to do things. I do not think about golf, dinner out, taking in a movie, cards with the guys, or doing things I could and should be doing. All the books and professionals explain that caregivers must take care of themselves. One of the things they may not be able to understand is that when a couple has been married this long and one partner is dying, the other is dying, too. I feel helpless, and I agonize over the fact that I cannot take care of her. I agonize over that fact that she is such an important part of me. We need to rewrite the books and retrain the professionals. My struggle will soon be how to take care of the half that must keep on living. It's an emotionally difficult thing to do. But tomorrow the first thing I will be asked is, "John, are you taking care of yourself?"

Alvetta was asleep on this day. She had only a few visitors. Ric and Kyla came in the afternoon. She was very glad to see them but did not talk. She is not talking at all now. Once in awhile she may say something and have a short conversation for a few moments. She looks at me and smiles. She doesn't want anyone to feel sorry for her. She appears to be very comfortable.

I can still read Alvetta's thoughts. I know when to ask people to leave. I know when she wants her bed up or down. I know when she wants music and not TV. I know when she wants a drink or when she just wants to hold hands.

I know she has only a limited amount of time to live. I know she wishes for everything to be in order but the cancer has really blunted her ability to think and plan. We talked about her funeral plans some time ago but did not finish. So with the help of family and friends we will do this part on our own and it will meet Alvetta's expectations. Alvetta would want it very elegant yet simple…a short funeral service. She also discussed some of her plans with Audrey.

At 5:15 p.m. her dinner arrived and I got her ready. She smiled as I tried to feed her. She was not very hungry. I will have to remember to order soup to go along with each meal in the future. Dinner is a repeat of lunch—Alvetta doesn't want to eat.

After dinner she fell asleep and I headed for home to a clean empty house. There was no noise. There was no one to say "'Dinner is ready" or "Can you clean up the dishes?" "What are we going to watch on TV tonight"? "You left your house shoes in a place where I could have tripped over them." God, how I miss her.

April 1, 2007

A year is both a long time and a short time. This deadly cancer has affected Alvetta over a year—a long time. The time since the cancer was discovered and the time given to her to live---6 months to a year—a short time.

When I arrived at Hospice, Audrey was there with her mother. "I Love Lucy" reruns were on but no one was watching. Audrey said Alvetta had not talked to her the entire time of her visit. Alvetta did not look right. Her eyes were glazed. Her skin was gray. I asked her if she was ok three or four times with no answer.

I went to find the nurse who stated she had had a good morning, a good bath and slowly ate her breakfast. Her sugar count was good and she was talking around 7:30 a.m. She fell asleep. Audrey left at 12:30 p.m. Alvetta ate about one tenth of her lunch and went back to sleep.

Ric, Shanon and Kyla arrived at 2:30 p.m. She opened her eyes for a few moments and went back to sleep. I tried to keep Kyla quiet but her noise did not wake up her grandmother.

Ric and family left and Alvetta's parents arrived. I had Alvetta sitting up and her eyes were open. I went for a walk. When I returned she was asleep. Her parents left before dinner arrived. She ate soup, half of a sandwich and a bite of pie.

April 2, 2007

I had set up a number of people to be with Alvetta on Tuesday April 3 because I had a trustee meeting. When I arrived at Hospice I knew I would not be going to the meeting. I didn't like the way she looked. The nurses and aides said they had to feed her breakfast. She had had a restful night but I could feel something that told me to stay close.

A minor problem about attending meetings when a loved one is dying is that one has to answer the same questions over and over. I know people really cared and were concerned but this is very hard on the caregiver. I also have this fear—and I know it's coming—that I will break down and fall apart. The time and place will not be of my choosing, but I hope and pray that it's with family and friends and close to home.

Alvetta slept most of the day. I helped her with lunch and dinner. She had lots of company—Pinky, Diane, Nana, Gramps, Percy, Cleo, Marcia. Alvetta talked some, but mostly slept.

Was it only a year ago today that we started the long trip home after her surgery in Florida?

April 3, 2007

It is a bright sunny day and I can feel spring in the air. Flowers are peeking out of the ground and birds are starting their concerts earlier each day. I know that Alvetta is in her final stages. She is sleeping more, talking less, pulling at the sheets, and staring blankly into space.

I arrived to find her bed completely wet. I thought her catheter was clogged, but she had spilled water on the bed while trying to drink it. She did not know she was wet.

The doctor came in to examine her and said that the tumor had picked up speed. I knew this. Alvetta had slowly been on the decline for the last few weeks. It was so slow that the average person could not see the change. Others held on to the hope that she was in a holding pattern and maybe a miracle would happen and she would recover.

Those who visited her today saw the change and did not linger. I could tell it in their eyes and the sound of their voices that they knew I was about to lose my loved one.

Nana and Gramps came by in the afternoon and stayed for a half hour. They seemed to know that Alvetta's time was very near. They watched her sleep, pull at her sheets, wake up, stare and fall right back to sleep. I saw the flickering flame in her eyes. She was comfortable. This has helped me to cope with her dying.

Thank God for Hospice, its staff and volunteers. Thank God for the ones who know that a place like this needed to exist. Thank God I understood enough to put her here.

I know that I will have a tough time dealing with the after effects of my wife's death. I know that I will need professional help. I know that I will need the prayers of others.

Now I feel Alvetta and I are in the perfect environment as the end process of living is taking place.

The flame is flickering.

We Look for Miracles

April 4, 2007

What a difference a day makes. Yesterday was bright, sunny and 77 degrees. Today, it's gray, cold and 37 degrees with a forecast of possible snow showers.

One of Alvetta's friends called to see if I had heard of a new type of radiation that was curing brain cancer. I tried to explain to her that Alvetta's Glioblastoma Multiforme had to be treated with surgery, chemotherapy and radiation. I told her that this type of tumor had tentacles, and even with the best treatment, the survival rate is very low. Age is another factor in surviving this tumor. I told her that the median survival is about 14 months. Alvetta's surgery was 12 months ago.

We all look for miracles. Ours is that Alvetta has lasted this long. We have had time to talk, plan, pray and get ready for a change in tomorrow.

I told the friend that we had started the grieving process and our prayers now are to give peace to Alvetta, her friends and family and special peace to her parents and the children. The friend asked, "What about you, John?" I told her my grieving started when the doctor told me a year ago that Alvetta's prognosis was terminal. I have had my fight with God. I was very angry. I was also very angry with myself. We married as children, just 16 and 19. I had promised to love and protect her from all harm. I promised to provide for her. Now I felt so helpless my belief in prayer has been challenged.

As I walked into her room today I knew it was time for my heart to start saying goodbye to my wife, as she is slowly dying each day.

Alvetta looked at me with a smile from her eyes and lips. I walked over and kissed her. She asked, "Where have you been?" and "Can we go home now?" I had to excuse myself for a few moments or I would have lost it.

She did well for a couple of hours. I walked the halls of Hospice, unable to sit, unable to think, unable to escape reality and unable to talk with anyone.

The Hospice staff understood. They saw me walking. They know her condition. They walk up to give me a bear hug that helps for a moment. Thank God for those angels on earth.

April 5, 2007

I am grieving because we are not educated, built or prepared to handle the loss of a loved one. Each day as I walk in to be with Alvetta, I know I am not prepared to see her go. I think to myself—is it better that death happens in a second? It has been also a year since I heard the doctors say that my wife had about six months to live.

The nurses had fed, washed and put clean clothes on Alvetta by the time I arrived. It's cold outside, but very warm inside. Alvetta greeted me with a smile.

We talked for a few minutes. This time it's about our first trip to Arkansas with Cathy and Ric—our first long drive outside of Ohio. Ric was still in diapers. We had borrowed my mother's car. That trip could have been a book in itself.

She pulled at her sheet and kept looking at her hands. She now does this even when she is talking to others and me. Sometimes, I think she is communicating with a Higher Power. She smiles for no reason. And, sometimes when I talk with her I think I have broken into her conversation with someone else.

I can sometimes feel the presence of someone else in the room when the two of us are very quiet and I have the CD player on very low. It's almost as if we have the capacity to enjoy the presence of God. This day was filled with friends, family flowers and cards. It was the Thursday before Easter.

Alvetta looked very comfortable. After lunch she wanted to sleep. I lowered her bed, brushed her hair and smoothed her sheets. I lowered the blinds, put a CD on low and let her drift off to another world. Her face was aglow and she smiled in her sleep. I knew she felt peace. I also knew that she was taking another step toward everlasting peace.

April 6, 2007

Alvetta's visitors started early today. Cards, flowers and telephone calls are in great numbers. Sister Mary, the ladies from the YMCA, a group from the church and others came not only to see Alvetta, but to also pray over her.

I was glad this took place early. Alvetta really enjoyed each and everyone, but she was ready to rest around 2 p.m. I read her cards to her. She doesn't read them herself anymore. She doesn't show any interest watching television or eating her meals.

I was glad that we talked a little before she fell asleep. It was almost in whispers. She told me that I looked tired and that I should be taking care of myself. We both said, "I love you." She looked at me with her eyes, heart and soul. I could feel and hear her thoughts. "Stay with me, love me, will you be ok?"

The tears welled up and she went on into her sleep. The room was very quiet except for the soft music. I hoped no one would show up at this moment. I could feel the presence of others in the room. I just sat, the two of us, and enjoyed this very special moment. I know that God sends his angels to us when someone is close to death. I could feel that there was something so special in the room. Even Sam the Hospice dog joined us. He found a corner and lay on the floor in the room and went to sleep.

These are the moments when coping with a loved one's dying is less difficult. I know that dying and death are not the same. I am attempting to deal with Alvetta's dying. I do not know if I can deal with Alvetta's death.

I know that I must get ready for the unknown. All the books on the subject may help some, but we are all different and handle things differently. It may be hard for me to accept that death means the end.

I will not see her again, talk to her again, tell her that I love her again or make plans for tomorrow…again.

Into the soul of my love
Wherein "I"
Am always with you
Even though I can't
Always hold your hand and walk
Or kiss you lips
In the dark of midnight
Or the laughter of sunlight.
My love can't ease our pain.
But it can promise faithfulness.

JCM, 1981

Loud Thoughts in a Quiet Room

April 7, 2007

Alvetta's mother is in the hospital. She was having dizzy spells so the doctor admitted her for a complete checkup. Her father is at home and we are checking on him. Tomorrow, he will celebrate his 92nd birthday.

I broke the news to Alvetta. I don't think she understood the impact of what I told her. She lives in another zone now. I repeated it a couple of times and hoped it sank in.

Later, I called her mother so that two of them could talk Hospice to hospital. They talked for a few minutes and I still couldn't tell if Alvetta really understood that her mother was in the hospital. Then the visitors, flowers and cards began to arrive. I walked the halls of Hospice and saw some patients leave never to return and new ones arrive. I introduced myself and tried make them feel comfortable. I assured them that they had made a wise choice in choosing Hospice.

Alvetta's room is now full of flowers, cards, family and friends. Long distance telephone calls have increased. She has touched so many people. I can tell they want her to know that before she leaves us. She smiles and I can see the tears well up in their eyes as they say goodbye to a very special lady. Then she sleeps. We return to our little world. Just the two of us.

April 8, 2007

Today is Easter and also Alvetta's father's birthday. He is 92. Alvetta's mother is in the hospital and Alvetta is in her 127th day in Hospice.

The weather is cold—snow is not on the ground. I did not attend church today. The house is empty. I did not want to watch television or listen to the radio. I just wanted to gather my thoughts for today. It is very difficult trying to reinvent myself each day.

Many television evangelists prey on the weak with their, "Send me your money and I will ask God to send you a blessing." Or, "I can cure you loved one of cancer". And even, "All you have to do is buy my prayer towel". They sucker in those who are at their weakest point and prey on the fear and superstition. I could write a book about them but that's another story for later.

This is Easter. The time of new birth. Alvetta is dying. I do not feel like celebrating on this day. Some may say that it's a blessing that it's her father's 92nd birthday and I should rejoice. I cannot.

I looked at Alvetta and tried to relive all the wonderful yesterdays. I know I must do that in order for me to keep going. I must hold on to the great memories of the past half-century. I recalled our early years when our income was as small as our first apartment and our budget of $10 a week for groceries was something we have laughed about ever since. So whenever the federal, state and local governments, or even another couple talked about the U.S. deficit, we could always say we knew about budgeting.

We always paid our bills first and then went shopping for food and for a year we were not to exceed $10 a week. We always saved for vacations before taking trips. Even when our children started to arrive, our method of balancing our budget never changed.

It's surprising the things one think about in a quiet room. A mind can wander in many directions about what is and what is yet to come. My faith is strong, but I do not know what it will be like when this is over. I know it took me years to forgive God over the loss of Cathy, our daughter. I really hurt for a long time when Bayyan, our grandson, passed away in his early teens. He had so much promise. He would have been whatever he wanted to be—teacher, professor, scientist, CEO —the list goes on.

It's 11:00 pm. and I am at home now. The house is empty, but clean. I can feel Alvetta's presence in every room. I walk in looking for a place to rest. I know if I fall asleep now I will be up in a few hours. So I go through the house looking for peace.

Each Day is a Blessing

The way of a fool is right in his own eyes: but he that hearkeneth unto counsel is wise.

Proverbs 12:15.

April 9, 2007

It is a gray, cold spring day. I arrive early and talked a long time with one of the doctors who were is concerned about me. I had made a statement that Hospice does an excellent job with the family and their needs but should provide a better program for the families whose loved ones don't die within the first 90 days.

She asked what kind of things they should be doing. I told her that I had made the statements on one of my really down days. I was speaking out because of my own emotional needs. I should have been reaching out for the resources that Hospice already has. I told her watching a loved one die slowly is one of the most challenging experiences one can face. It is frustrating, lonely and overwhelming.

For me it is a feeling of helplessness and guilt. I also feel neglected. I do not know what to ask for or what my needs are. So I criticized the system that is doing a super job. I know it's essential that I reach out and find support. Anyone living under these circumstances should be yelling for help. The resources that the family needs are part of the Hospice program. All I have to do is ask.

Alvetta had company and was awake this Monday morning. She did not say a word. Her eyes told me all I needed to know. I brushed her hair, smoothed her sheets, got fresh water and ice for her. I turned off the TV, put music on and raised her bed.

I then talked with her day nurse. She told me that Alvetta did not eat much for breakfast. She was confused and asked for the bedpan constantly. She no longer knows if and when she needs it.

After her company left, Alvetta fell right back to sleep. Oh! My God! She is getting weaker each day. Friends call daily to let me know that I should call them if I need them and I know they mean just that. My problem is that I don't know what to ask for. I know they want a strong suggestion on how they can benefit us the most.

Alvetta had to be awakened for lunch. One of her friends was there to feed her and give me a break. I returned 45 minutes later and she was still eating. Her eyes told me, "Don't leave me for lunch again. I want you to feed me." I told her that after her friend had left that I would feed her from then on. She smiled.

When dinnertime arrived I fed her. She ate well and fell asleep. I started for the clean, empty house and started the process of reinventing myself for tomorrow.

April 10, 2007

The sun came out for a few minutes. It started its path across the sky and disappeared before noon.

The doctor was in to see Alvetta with a few student doctors. He wanted me to know that he and the nurses are getting more and more concerned about Alvetta's failing condition. He gave her a very thorough examination. The left side of her face showed an increased amount of swelling. Even with the help of others, her desire to eat had dwindled by 60% or more. Her attention span was down to a few minutes at best.

He asked me how I was doing. I told him I was already starting to use good memories to make it through the day. Every time I start to despair would think of a funny time from our past.

Today, one happy memory I recalled was when we were singing a song in bed. This had to be in the late 1960s. While we were singing blues song 'Father Brown", Ric and Cathy quietly crossed into the room and recorded us on their new tape recorder. The next morning at the breakfast table they played it back. We all laughed at that for days. Then we wondered what else they had recorded in the privacy of our bedroom. We would laugh about this for years.

I know already that the good times and the bad times of our life together will help me to get on with the rest of my life without a person I had been with for now over 75% of my life. Life without Alvetta—Wow!!!

April 11, 2007

It is still wet and cold. A mixture of rain and snow greet me as I arrive for my daily 6:30 a.m. workout at the YMCA. These trips to Hospice give me time to ask questions of myself. On my mind this morning is "What do I do after Alvetta? If I need help, where to I go? Whom do I reach out to? What major changes should I expect in my lifestyle? Will I be able to handle the emotional shifts that will be coming?"

I arrived at Hospice and some of the answers to my questions may have been answered. The priest from our church let me know that he would be around when I needed him. Then two Hospice volunteers walked into Alvetta's room. Both had lost their spouses. They said hello to Alvetta and her parents. They asked me to walk outside of the room so that they could speak with me. One told me that he had lost his wife to cancer and was introduced to Hospice. After her death he retired and became a volunteer. The woman had also lost her mate and was also a new volunteer for Hospice. The gentleman told me about a program put on by Hospice for those that had lost their loved ones and that it would be starting in June.

Alvetta's condition is slowly going downhill. Each day she doesn't remember what occurs around her. She smiles and is very comfortable. She sleeps longer and deeper. She no longer feeds herself or asks for the bedpan. The "10 minutes only" visitors' sign is out and I am enforcing it.

She is so precious to so many people that they come to see her time and time again. Others will not come. They want to remember her in her grand style. The right dress, the right colors, hair cut to perfection, her makeup on as if an artist had done the job. Just the right amount of jewelry.

I remember our trips together: New York, San Francisco, Rome or Boston. We would walk into a shop or store, whether it was an art gallery, jewelry store or car dealership and the salesperson would take care of us as if we had a lot of dollars. This was the sophisticated style that Alvetta could portray. She also knew art, music, flowers, jewelry and designers and could talk in a manner that would impress the salesperson. If we bought an item and returned to the store years later they would remember this lady of class.

I could write volumes on our shopping trips, but that's another story at a later time.

April 12, 2007

The weather is still wet and cold. It is the kind of day you wish you could curl up in front of the fire with a hot mug of coffee, a good book and soft jazz playing in the background. But I know what my day is going to be like so I clean up the house and head for Hospice.

I talked with the nurse before I went in. She told me that Alvetta had a whirlpool bath and a massage and would be resting for a while. She was right. Alvetta slept the whole morning. I had to wake her up for lunch.

After lunch she went back to sleep and my mind turned to end of life concerns. I seem to have a sixth sense in knowing that each day we lose a lot more of her. It's hard now because of the lack of conversation. For almost 52 years the two of us have always talked and made plans. Now we are the largest crises of our lives and my partner cannot participate in the process. We have some details of how we want her funeral, but there is so much to do. I know I should ask the family for more input and share some of this burden. It is overwhelming when one has to plan alone.

April 13, 2007

We have sunshine today and it's warmer. Alvetta is asleep. The nurse says she has she has been this way since breakfast. Alvetta's urine output is down which is not a good sign.

Alvetta woke up for lunch. The nurses cleaned her up and she was ready to eat. I could tell the day was going to be one of her better ones. She ate most of her lunch but I had to feed and encourage her to eat more.

The only down of the day was a call from a friend of the family who had not talked to Alvetta in five or six years and was upset and angry with me for having moved Alvetta into the Hospice facility. She felt I should take her home. The family friend said that if she were well she would come over and help me take care of her.

Wow. One has to be strong. People who mean well call me and neither of us knows what to say. This person had not visited her, and had never called about her condition before, but the conversation was really upsetting.

Alvetta did not fall asleep after dinner. She watched the birds outside her window attacking the bird feeder. The sun was out and she was talking. As always, she asked me how everyone was doing. I wanted to ask her questions, but she was in charge, so I let her talk. She asked things like, "Who's in the hall?", "Is there a new person next door?" Then she asked me if we could to go a movie tonight. I knew to just to let her talk and enjoy the moment.

Nana, Gramps and Percy walked in. Alvetta was sitting in bed and smiling. Her steroids had been cut and her face was not as swollen. Nana sat next to her. They held hands and made small talk. Gramps just smiled sat back, and enjoyed the moment with his wife and their baby.

I knew this was a good day! I thanked God because I know what tomorrow and the next day would bring. Now my mind must linger on the here and now. Tomorrow is tomorrow and today is right now. I must enjoy it.

After her company left and she ate dinner, we watched the sunset in silence. I let her bed down. She was tired. She wanted to relax and escape into sleep. That was ok because this was a good day.

⋙My Hero⋘

April 14, 2007

If you love someone you should tell that person every day. The moment can vanish had you may not have a chance. Don't be afraid to express yourself over and over again.

Those were the words that I said to Alvetta as I walked into her room. I did not like the way she looked; nothing really stood out but I just had a feeling that things were not right.

The nurse had spent a lot of time getting Alvetta ready. She wore sunglasses, had one of her best gowns and one of the cutest hats on. Even with her hat and a smile on her face I knew as I walked in the room that life was leaving her. Each moment of rest she could get would add another minute of her time to be with us. I knew that for the next few of days, I would be very protective of her time. Others might not understand but I will ask them to shorten their visits and let only a few in the room at a time.

Her lunch and dinner were both a task for her to consume. I had to feed her very slowly. She only enjoyed the soup and a small sip of water. I did not want to leave her but I knew that in a few days I would be there both day and night. So I started for home to make all of my calls to update friends and family and to spend the night with our memories and all of our yesterdays. I knew that I would try to recapture the very best memories and that if I could, then maybe I could sleep tonight so that I could face tomorrow.

April 15, 2007

It is snowing this morning! What a strange spring! The tender flower buds look for somewhere to hide and the birds are wonder if they should return south.

This morning was the same it's been for a long time now. Sundays are usually the days that Alvetta has a lot of company after church. Audrey was the first to arrive followed all day by friends, family, social club members and her sorority sisters. Alvetta enjoyed them all and as she grew tired, I would have to empty the room and let her take naps before the next group would arrive.

The last couple of days the nurses had make an all out effort to make her look better, using scarves and hats and her best gowns. The room was full of flowers, cards and also a number of books on healing.

The last of her guests left around 5 p.m. At 5:30 p.m. I fed her dinner and she ate better than I thought she would. Still it was not like she had done a week ago.

Sunday was a good day for Alvetta. But it's just not the same. She is not asking to go home. She just smiles, sleeps and talks occasionally. Each day she will say something funny to the nurses and they will laugh the entire shift. Her sense of humor lifts them up. She is really my hero. She does not complain. She would be a hero to others if they could see how she is living her final days.

We live in a world of whiners. They whine about everything. We even make them bigger than life by watching them on TV. We elect them to political office. We call them senators, congressmen, governors and presidents. We call them CEO's and blue collar workers. They find ways every day to complain. Alvetta is a fighter for the most important thing there is —life—and does not complain. She is my hero.

Cherishing the Golden Moments

April 16, 2007

Spring is trying to turn things around. We had 2 days of sunshine. It is about 11:30 p.m. I am trying to capture today before I go to sleep. I am so tired at the end of the day but I am not going to miss a day at Hospice. My social life is my 8 to 10 hours with Alvetta each day.

She asked me to be with her. I do not want her to be alone at the end. A few times I have gone back after midnight just to spend a few more moments with her.

Today I looked back over our almost 52 years of marriage. I remember wonderful days full of joy, hope, purpose and a true sense of each other. Today, I looked at the pain of separation which death will bring. I know that I am blessed and that we had an exciting life together. Now I must start to have a whole new life style at age 70.

This Monday Alvetta had a number of visitors: Shanon and Kyla, Nana and Gramps. Lenora and Jill, Norma and Percy. She slept with a new glow that lit up the room. She will wake for a while, smile and then return to sleep.

I can hear peace in her voice. I can see peace on her face. I can feel peace in her heart. I also pray to God for peace in her soul.

April 17, 2007

You can read all the books; talk to all the professionals, have the greatest of faith. But I will tell you: There is no way you can be prepared to watch a loved one slowly die.

Each day Alvetta loses a little of herself. She does not like the taste of food. Her appearance is of no concern to her. She sleeps all day. Her skin has lost some of its color. Her skin is moist to the touch and her muscles are starting to turn soft. Her eyes are not as bright or as wide open now. Her smile is starting to fade.

She holds my hand and doesn't want to let go. She falls asleep and still holds on as if she lets go, she will also depart.

The Hospice staff is talking to me more, hugging more and asking me if I am taking care of myself. One of the social workers asked me about my plans for the future and if I could leave Toledo for a while.

They are also spending a lot of time in Alvetta's room. They clean her up, change her clothes, laugh and talk with her and are always asking her if they can get her anything.

The visitors continue to come as if they have to make certain they have had a chance to say goodbye. They laugh and talk but most leave with tears in their eyes.

April 18, 2007

Alvetta's father is in the hospital. He was to have an outpatient procedure but his tests were not good so he will be kept there for a couple of days. Gramps is 92 and has a number of health problems. This is the news that I plan to carry to Alvetta today.

When I arrived at Hospice the doctor walked to Alvetta's room with me. She sat and asked if I had noticed some of the changes in Alvetta. I told her I had and explained that I had noted the lack of eating, increased sleeping and the increased swelling in her left side. I also mentioned that her eyes were different, that she could not focus and could not communicate at length

She asked me to walk with her. She said they had noticed a large change each day and for me to prepare for the worse. The nurses had talked about her lack of response. I told her I would be spending the night fairly soon.

It's hard to accept the facts sometimes even when you know what the facts are. Each time I think I am ready; I am faced with knowing that Alvetta's days are numbered. I let my emotions come through. Deep feelings are making it to the surface. I know that I am going to be basket case once she leaves me. All the time I thought I was strong and would be able to handle whatever the future would bring—now I don't know. Life without her may not be a life at all.

April 19, 2007

The head doctor wants to see me when I arrive. Each day I am going earlier and stay later. The doctor wants examine Alvetta with me in the room. She does not respond to him well. He asks her questions and she looks at him, then me, and smiles. He said it was time to take away the pills as Alvetta had declined in the past week. He suggests I get our religious leader in while she can still communicate.

The nurses and staff on each shift took turns in talking and hugging. They kept asking me if I was ok. One nurse, who is very close to Alvetta, talked about her own parents. Her father knew that her mother was dying and they did everything they could to help him get ready. For months they had all the professionals and religious leaders helping but when she died, he fell apart. She told me, "John, you are a very strong man, but get ready for the worse." We can tell how much you love each other and that your loss will be something you can prepare for."

The second shift heard about Alvetta's condition. They came down and also talked to me. They talked about this very beautiful, highly educated sophisticated lady who had never lost her dignity. In the face of death, she was still a lady.

It is always a great feeling when others discover what you already know. Alvetta is a lady in the true sense.

April 20, 2007

The sun was out. The weather was finally starting to look like spring. Gramps is still at the hospital but even at his age we have no big concerns. He looks good and will possibly be home by Monday.

Alvetta, however, was having problems. I had called our priest and explained to his answering service about Alvetta's condition and the doctors' concerns. I asked him to meet me at Hospice. We arrived at the same time.

The doctor was outside Alvetta's door and the three of us sat down and talked. The doctor was very concerned over the change in her over the last three days. The priest wanted to meet with her privately. Fifteen to twenty minutes he came out of her room and said she did not respond to anything he said but he could tell from her eyes that she knew he was in the room. He made his final prayers with her and gave her communion. We talked about God being close by and we could feel His presence. This happens when death is close.

The nurses decided to unhook Alvetta's bed and roll her outside into the sunshine. She loves the sun and for a few moments her smiles were as warm as the weather and her eyes as clear as the sky. I am now praying to God for a few more moments, not a few more days. These final moments are precious for Alvetta and me.

April 21, 2007

Alvetta is a warrior! Today she is laughing, talking, and telling me what to do! Yesterday she slept. Today she is sitting up and waiting to go outside. She eats her lunch and dinner better than she has in some time. She talks to all of her visitors. Sometimes she was confused, but she tries to communicate.

Her face was alive and aglow. She could not wait for us to push her bed outside into the fresh air and sunshine. The birds were singing and the beautiful pool and water fountain made for a perfect environment. The Hospice staff came out to see her. She had on a light blue denim hat and sunglasses. With her cranberry red gown, she was again the lady of fashion with the smile to go with it.

The sun was behind her and I could see the halo around her head as she talked. She said she loved the setting. For over an hour she enjoyed life as it should be enjoyed. Later, she will battle death, but for these golden moments, she will enjoy life.

As I looked at her all of the so-called large problems of the world became small: wars, gun control, abortion, global warming, healthcare and the budget. Alvetta in the sunshine, being full of life, letting me know what is really important.

A Troubled Heart

April 22, 2007

The days overwhelm me and I know they are more so for Alvetta who has been fighting this terrible disease for over a year. The governments of the world should wake up and face the real terrorists—disease. They should wake up and seek out all of the diseases of the world and resolve to find a cure. People die everyday from sickness that we could stop if we put our resources together.

She was awake for me as I entered the room on this bright warm Sunday morning. She had on one of her favorite gowns, a little scarf and that natural glow of her skin. She looked to be at peace with the world.

I was surprised that she talked to me. I was also surprised that she ate a little of her lunch. I knew one of the reasons that she was eating less was that she had to be fed. Here was a person who has always been self sufficient and independent. Now she has to be humble. She needed help to do the smallest things.

I know what some of her thoughts were, so I took advantage of our blessings and spent the time talking. She tells me that she is worried about me. She holds my hand and strokes my arm and asks me if I am ok. I fought back the tears and tried to assure her that I was all right.

Although we have been married over 50 years, our relationship has grown stronger over the last 11 months. Our faith has also grown. Alvetta is at peace and that comes from her faith in God and His promises. I know this and it sustains me. Even with our increased faith it does not bring full understanding of how I will face life after Alvetta. I know the verse "Let not your heart be troubled," but it is.

Life without Alvetta

Alvetta is Loved

April 23, 2007

Gramps is having some problems with his pacemaker. As they made some adjustments, his heart stopped. He is now 100% dependent on it. He has problems with his kidneys and prostate. He has gone through a number of very painful procedures.

Alvetta was having a good day. The nurses had her sitting up with a scarf on her head and dressed in a beautiful gown.

I am surprised that she wants to talk. She asked me if I had made plans for us to visit the Villages in Florida. I asked if she remembered us going there for a week. We played golf, went swimming met people from Bowling Green State University and had a wonderful villa to live in. She looks confused but wants to know if we can do it again.

By this time some of her sorority members had arrived and she talked to them. I used to always leave the room and walk the halls to give visitors a chance to talk. Now 15 minutes is long enough and most of her visitors know when I walk back into the room, it is time to wrap up their visit.

Alvetta is loved. Each day we end up with some visitor for the first time or a card or telephone call from people that I have not seen or even known. They send their best. They pray for us.

The prayers of so many must make a difference because Alvetta has lasted longer than the doctors thought she would. We know now "Its not their time, it's God's time." I received an invitation to dinner and as I drove home my mind was not to go, but friends and family talked me into it.

So I went. Three of the guests had their spouses. The priest from our church was present. It turned out to be the perfect evening. The food, the wine and the company made it a great break. Lots of the talk consisted of reflections of Alvetta.

A Student Remembers

Letters from Heidi

Dear Mr. Moore:

    I was very sorry to hear that Mrs. Moore is in Hospice. I hadn't heard from her in a while and had a feeling that she might not be feeling well. Thank you so much for letting me know. She has always been such a strong person and I know that she must have given this illness a big fight.

    I have written her a short note. I was wondering if you wouldn't mind reading it to her for me. It is just a few things that I have been thinking about over the past few months and would like her to know.

    I hope that your prayers are answered and that you will have another Christmas together. I will be thinking of you both and will say many prayers.

Love Heidi (Gorn)

Dear Mrs. Moore,

    I just wanted to write you a short note and remind you of all the lives you have touched over the years by being such a wonderful teacher. You were always my favorite teacher and I was very lucky to have you for both first and sixth grades.

    It seems like we always had a special friendship and I will never forget that. You are such a wonderful, smart person.

I was sorry to hear that you have not felt well for some time now. I know that you will be a special teacher no matter where life takes you. I hope that my child will be lucky enough to experience what it's like to have a favorite teacher and to always remember him or her, just like I will always remember you.

Love and hugs, Heidi

Heidi Gorn

A Simple Prayer

April 23, 2007

I stop by the hospital to see Gramps, Alvetta's father. He is ready to go home. I do not like to see him in the hospital, but it is a blessing for Nana. She waits on him around the clock, so his hospitalization gives her a few days of rest and a break. This may be a short one, but one well needed.

Alvetta was asleep when I arrived. The nurse said she did not each much but was in a great mood and talked with them. I let her sleep and rolled my chair close to her bed. I turned on some soft music and just watched her sleep.

She woke up smiling and waved at me. She wanted something to drink. Afterwards, I told her about her father and that he would be going home in the next couple of days. I brushed her hair, smoothed her bed, washed her hands and dressed her in one of the scarves I had brought from home.

Nana and Percy arrived and are glad to see her sitting up and smiling. They kiss and talk. Alvetta tells them that the next time they should bring her father.

The last couple of days have been less confusing for Alvetta. She is sitting up and talking to people. She looks great. Alvetta has had another wonderful day. She eats a little more for dinner. Each day is a miracle. The prayers are working. Each day is precious. Alvetta helps me to be thankful for each moment. I leave hoping I can have another day with Alvetta.

April 25, 2007

This is not a good day. The nurses let me know that Alvetta ate very little for breakfast and is getting harder to wake up. I know after her two great days I should prepare myself for a deeper decline, but it's hard.

The weather had turned cold and rainy once more. It set the mood for the day. I grabbed a book and went to the big reclining chair in the room. I did not want to talk to anyone. My feelings were very sensitive. This was not a time to be around a lot of people. I hoped the weather would keep people away.

Alvetta slept until I woke her up for lunch. In the past she would wake up when the nurses entered the room. Now she isn't doing that. A new patient was admitted and a large family came in with him. His room is next to hers. With all the noise, sometimes very loud, nothing seems to bother her.

As she came out of her sleep I could tell she was confused. I raised her bed and got her ready for lunch. She looked at me and went back to sleep, so I had to start over again. With a lot of encouragement I got her to eat a little of her lunch. She looked at me with her eyes and asked me to lay her back down. Even before I did so, she was asleep. She opened her eyes for a few seconds to see Nana but went back to sleep.

She slept until the nurse woke her up to check her sugar levels and give her medication. To me, this signaled the beginning of the end. I cannot see her bouncing back after today. She has done it so many times in the last 150 days, but I feel, this time, it will not happen. As I drove home, I started making plans to spend the night. I will pack the car this time—just in case.

April 26, 2007

Last night I said a simple prayer: "God let your will be done, and I will accept it."

I had listened to professionals, reading materials on death and grieving and even reviewed motivational tapes and CDs to help me at this time, but only one thing, that simple prayer gave me peace.

As I sat with Alvetta while she slept, I felt a peace that was so relaxing it comforted me. It let me know that I was going to be strong enough to handle tomorrow. It was the most amazing feeling. The next thing I realized was the tears was flowing from my face. They weren't tears of sadness but tears of hope, peace and fulfillment. This went on for ten or more minutes, but the feeling of peace lasted the whole day.

I will have to repeat my simple prayer every day: "God, let your will be done, and I will accept it."

Footprints on Our Hearts

When I retired from Bowing Green State University one of the students gave me a plaque that stated: "Some people come into our lives and quietly go. Others stay for a while, leave their footprints on our hearts and we are never the same."

Alvetta has truly left her footprint on all of us. She has really left it on the Hospice staff. Even the staff not assigned to her drop in to talk, check her gowns and look at pictures of friends and family. They want to know what she was like before she got sick.

They talk about her mannerisms. She is a classy lady. They comment on her beautiful smiles. They say they would die for her hands and fingernails. They talk about her beautiful gowns and comment that she must have a wonderful wardrobe. They call her a "breath of fresh air". She never complains. She is always a lady.

The Nurses Tell Their Story

I worked the 11 p.m. – 7 a.m. shift. While taking care of Alvetta during the night, she always had a smile on her face. Even if she needed to be awakened. Alvetta had pink cheeks and was a beautiful lady. She enjoyed talking about her family, the visitors she had that day and what was on TV. She always had colorful gowns to wear. She did laugh and made me laugh at times. I will remember her.

Mary Ann Windischman-Auld

Alvetta always had a smile. Even if she wasn't sure she knew you, she would smile engagingly and give a little wave. She was beautiful, but her face just lit up when she smiled and her eyes sparkled! She just loved people! She was a delight!

Amey Raihala, RN

Talking With Our Eyes

April 27, 2007

It is another cold, wet day in Toledo. Spring has disappeared for a while. I wonder how Hospice of Northwest Ohio continues to find quality people to work for them. Alvetta has a new nurse today. She is as wonderful and as caring as all the rest. She takes care of Alvetta as if she is her only patient.

She tells me Alvetta did not eat any breakfast. She could not keep her from going back to sleep. She had to carefully feed her. She did not want her choking. I told her I would try to get Alvetta to eat at lunchtime, but I know I will simply let her sleep.

The weather kept her visitors away until after lunch. I woke her up 20 minutes before lunch arrived. I washed her face and hands and brushed her hair. I turned on the TV, which helped her prepare for lunch. She had seafood soup, a tuna sandwich, fruit and ginger ale. She ate one-third of the sandwich, two spoonfuls of soup and sipped a little ginger ale.

The nurses came in after lunch, cleaned her up, and rearranged her in the bed. She went right to sleep and slept until the afternoon nurse showed up to check her readings. At this time her visitors started to come. She was able to talk to them for a while. As the visitors arrived she was ready with a big smile. All would tell her how much they enjoyed her smile and how beautiful she was. She never got tired of listening to them.

After dinner and after all visitors had left for home and family, a feeling came over for that was utter isolation and depression. The room was quiet. Alvetta was asleep. I listened to music for a while and dreaded the drive home.

No book, no sermon, no DVD or CD can prepare one for the loneliness of an empty house. When one has shared a home with someone for over a half-century one cannot get used to an empty house.

My friends and family all want to help, but they have gone home and I have this feeling that no one really cares. At this moment I don't think anyone can capture the utter feeling of pure isolation. This is a lower level of pure despair.

Then with the isolation and despair comes fear. This is the fear that I am truly alone. My faith is challenged—does God really care? After over 50 years I wonder what life will be without Alvetta.

April 28, 2007

The sun was out for a little while but a sweater and light jacket feel good. Spring where are you?

The calls I got this morning! "Can I see her?" "How is she doing?" "How are you?" "How is her father?" "Are you taking time for yourself?" "What can I do to help?"

This is the same almost everyday. Loved ones call for an update. I wish I had my own newspaper each day to print out the latest news alert about Alvetta. I have to keep telling myself that the loving and caring want to know. Please, John, I warn myself. Do not say anything that you will have to apologize for later.

Alvetta has been in Hospice for 174 days. I am completely worn out. I get up early so I can have quiet moments to myself before the telephone starts to ring. A hot cup of coffee. The newspaper. A walk out on the deck. A few minutes to escape reality. Then a hot shower and a change of clothes. This sets my thoughts and body for another day.

This Saturday was no change. The nurses, as they tended to do nowadays, reached me before I reached Alvetta's room with the updates—did not eat well—would not take her pills—could not focus—are you ok!!!

Alvetta slept until I woke her up for lunch. Pasta, salad, soup, bread and dessert. I am now trying a combination of foods hoping she will eat something. She does, but only a small amount. She smiles. I talk with not much response on her part. I talk anyway. I tell her how beautiful she is. How her hat, gown and scarf look. I tell her what a lovely day it is and it's warming up. I look at her and she is already asleep. She remains this way until the shifts change and they need her readings.

I was glad her visitors showed up before her dinner and she was able to smile and talk for a little while. They drove up from Florida just to have a few minutes with her. The stated they would not be back. They wanted to remember her as the elegant lady that she is.

It's words like that that overwhelm me. It also helps me to understand that whatever changes she goes though I will be there with her. She tells me everyday that she wants me close by. People tell me that I need time off and that they will take care of her. The voices I hear from Alvetta's eyes are, "Do not leave me—do not forsake me—I do not want to be left alone and I do not want to die alone."

After all these years we can talk in a way that only we can understand.

April 29, 2007

The sun is up and it promises to be a nice day. The high should reach 70 with no chance of rain. I sit at the kitchen table finishing my cup of coffee, getting ready for another day with Alvetta. As I sit looking out of the window, my mind shifts back to an earlier day of Alvetta's life. Her life as a five-year-old living in the Brand Whitlock complex. This was a community of 375 apartments that were federally funded and comprised entirely of African-American families.

I can hear her now playing with the children. Her mother kept her neat and clean and in the in the latest little girl fashions. She loved to play, run and ride her tricycle. It was a community of families. One always felt loved and protected by the elders, but still had to fight for respect for the other children—that's another story.

Alvetta was glad to see me when I arrived at Hospice. The nurse said she ate only a little breakfast and refused to take her medication. I talked her into it. I asked her why she did not want to take her meds—she would not tell me.

Today's lunch was one of her favorites. Oven-fried chicken, mashed potatoes, corn, rolls and butter. She ate a little of each. She told me she wanted to sleep for a while. I told her that when she awakened we could take her outside in her bed. The weather was perfect.

Two of the nurses pulled me aside and wanted to know if I wanted to take a day in this great weather to play golf. I told them I would have a lot of time to play golf in the future. I thanked them for caring.

Alvetta woke up and we rolled her outside with her hat, sunglasses and covered from the bright sun. Her visitors arrived and were glad to see her outside. She was beaming and really enjoyed the outdoors. After everyone left for the day—friends, family, godchildren and church members, Alvetta was ready for a nap.

I sat and tried to relax. It is really a hard job in sitting and waiting and thinking and grieving. I wondered how much longer she would hold on. Yesterday the woman next door passed away. Alvetta has now been at Hospice longer than any patient currently there.

I have tried to put everything in place, but some things I don't want to. I guess deep down inside there is this small feeling of hope. That a miracle could happen and Alvetta would return home and would resume our lives. Even though deep down I know that our time with Alvetta is coming to an end.

April 30, 2007

The sun is shining and we have good news. Alvetta's father is coming out of the hospital. He will need a walker. He is having problems with one of his legs but he is 92 and still alive.

I walked into Hospice and looked for doctors. Alvetta's eyes have been red for the last couple of days. I want the doctors to tell me it is a sign of the growing tumor or something in the air from spring. I also call Shanon to come in tomorrow and do Alvetta's nails. These are the nails the nurses say they would die to have.

This is a good day for Alvetta. She is looking out of the window and tells me hello as I walk in. I let her know her father will be going home today and one of her Red Hatters will be joining her for lunch.

One of her sorority sisters arrived at the same time I did. They laughed and talked but she respected our time and stayed just for a few minutes. Then a friend of one of our neighbors whose wife was admitted to Hospice a few days ago also stops in. I told Alvetta that she was in a room across the hall. That's when reality set in. Alvetta does not recognize him and forgot I had told her about his wife.

A few of the nurses that have been reassigned also stop in to see her. They stated they had stopped before, but she was always asleep.

I called her mother so Alvetta could talk with her. This really lifted both of their spirits.

The nurses had a rough time getting Alvetta to take her medication again. She simply refused. I had success a couple of times but it took me 15 to 20 minutes of begging, coaching and trying to slip it into her food.

She is still eating only about one-fifth of her meals. I order a number of items hoping a variety will help. She has a little of each. She is not drinking as much. Her sugar readings are starting to climb again.

It's days like today that I wonder why I put her into Hospice almost 150 days ago. Then I do a reality check and know I did the right thing. She is receiving the very best care.

May 1, 2007

The weather is wet and cold. I made all the calls to family and friends to update them on Alvetta's condition. If I don't do this at least once a week they will call me at all hours. Sunday is Nurse's Day so I pick up a few cards for each shift. They have been just wonderful.

Alvetta's list of guests started early, but they did not get a chance to talk to her because she has been sleeping all day. I had to wake her up for Shanon to do her nails.

She had guests the night before. One of her out-of-town godchildren stopped in and had a wonderful conversation with her but she doesn't remember.

Alvetta still is not eating or taking her medication. She talks, but it is very confused. I still listen to just to try to capture wonderful moments of the past. My mind today shifts to our Alaskan cruise. It was just the two of us and we had a great time. The August weather required a sweater and jacket. The food, the scenery, the smell of the ocean and the people we met on board were the many highlights of the trip.

Alaska is a beautiful place. At first Alvetta did not want to go. She wanted to go to sandy beaches with tropical islands and wear all sorts of swimsuits.

Alaska did not offer any of those but what it did offer would equal them. We wanted to do this trip again, but for two weeks, not just one.

Cherishing the Moments

May 2, 2007

I went to the YMCA this morning like I do every Monday, Wednesday and Friday. I like to work out for a few hours. It is my only escape. I push myself and it allows me to relax for a few minutes and live in another world.

This is very hard. I am 70 years old and for the last 51 1/2 years I had only one true partner and I know that in a very short time I will lose her.

Each day the truth reality hits me that Alvetta is terminally ill. She has been sick since the first of March, 2006. She is now receiving end of life care from Hospice of Northwest Ohio. She started home care on October 17, 2006 with a diagnosis of Glioblastoma Multiforme, a very rare, but terminal brain cancer. The doctors all stated there was no hope.

Each day that Alvetta lives is a special blessing from God. She has beaten all odds. She is strong, determined and positive. I take it one day at a time. I do not measure our time left in days. I measure our time in minutes and enjoy every seconds we have together. She was a model to the people who complain day in and day out about each little setback.

As I watch her in this very difficult time, it's hard to know where she gets the power to go on. She smiles, she laughs and she jokes with the nurses and always asks if I am ok. I just say, "Yes, Alvetta!"

May 3, 2007

This is not a good day. Alvetta's father is back in the hospital. They just admitted a baby next door to Alvetta and a person died on the other side. I got to visit our friend who lives in our community. She's been here just a few days and in that time she looks like she may not make it to the next day.

Alvetta is so confused. She does not know were she is. I tell her she is in Hospice, but she doesn't understand.

Her good friend Diane arrived and laughed and joked but Alvetta is some place in the past.

She looks great! Her makeup is in place and her gown and scarf look great. The room is full of flowers and stuffed teddy bears. The birds are eating from the bird feeders outside her window. Sam, the Hospice dog stops in every hour to check on her and see what crumbs of food are available.

I am really trying to pace myself and save my energy. I know I must stay in control. I am so tired and frustrated. I try to laugh about something every day. Sometimes what has happened from the day lifts me to a funny moment in the past. It calms me down and helps me just to make it through the day. I have always been a strong believer in the power of laughter.

I hear crying from the families of loved ones nearby. They seem to be passing each day. I want to comfort them, but the hard part is that most of them are here for only a few moments before their loved one passes away.

How many times have I heard them say, "I wish I had known about Hospice before", or "My loved one and the family could have really enjoyed the final days." I know in my heart that Hospice is "not about giving up, but planning to give" the best of life to a loved one's last days on earth.

Alvetta is here and each day we try as best we can to enjoy her final days. My Lady, Alvetta.

May 4, 2007

The day is sunny but cool. The neighbors are coming home from their winter breaks and are asking about Alvetta. They didn't think she would be around for their return. She is. She is smiling and looking as beautiful as ever. I will take a few more gowns and scarves to her today.

A few of our neighbors stopped in to see Alvetta. I also send thank you cards to a few for the flowers. I can tell the tumor is growing.

Alvetta's actions and confusion lets me know she doesn't understand where she is.

She is in pain now, but not from the tumor. There is a problem with the catheter.

Through all of this she is still a lady: her mannerisms, the tone of her voice, the way she looks with all she has had to deal with. Those who enter her room know they are in the presence of a very special lady.

Some of the teachers she taught with came to visit and were laughing at some of Alvetta's' rules. At their morning gatherings she would tell all: "Do not touch the food unless you plan to eat it". "No sampling and putting it back on the plate"! She also told them she did not believe in dress down days. The students should always see the teachers at their best.

May 5, 2007

The sun was out but it is still cold and windy. Gramps is still in the hospital. This is a busy day for Alvetta. Members from two of her clubs show up. First there were the members of the Toledo Chapter of Delta Sigma Theta sorority. They were all dressed in red. This was their special Saturday. They put on a large fundraiser each May called "Breakfast for My Lady." They left there and stopped in to see Alvetta. Someone from the organization shows up almost every other day.

The next group was the Toledo Chapter of Charms, Inc. A few of them who have not been to visit her stopped in. This is another group that stops in two or three times a week.

Alvetta is not doing well at all. She is sleeping very soundly. At one time a person could walk into the room and she would awaken. Now we have to shake her to get her ready for meals, bath and medications.

The nurses do all they can to make her look good. Her makeup, scarf and special gown and hair are all arranged to perfection. The room is filled with fresh flowers and a large numbers of stuffed animals as well as pictures of friends and family are on display.

The highly trained volunteers have provided Alvetta with comfort and companionship. They bring fresh water, sit down and chat at the right moment. hey give out several lap quilts and comfort pillows. They are wonderful people who truly care.

I am doing my best to keep up a front for the family and myself. At the end of the day I am so tired. Not from just sitting all day. Now it's more of worrying about tomorrow and what is to come.

May 6, 2007

This is Nurse's Day. I pick up three cards and add a note for each shift. Most of them did not know it was Nurse's Day. For a few moments I am their hero.

Today is quiet. A few people stopped in to see Alvetta. It was a nice quiet day.

I sat alone most of the day with her. It was not a good day. I can tell you now that a patient' end of life experience is one that is equally shared by the partner, family, or caregiver. These 13 months have been the hardest ones of my entire life. I thank God that at the right moment he always gives me someone with an open heart, who is deeply concerned about my well-being.

Over these 13 months I felt the full emotional roller coaster. There are times I am at peace with Alvetta's impending death and the life (long life) we have shared. At other times, I feel the fear of change and loneliness, danger, guilt and helplessness.

People say: "Pray and God will hear your prayers". "He will give you comfort and peace". What happens if what I want is for Alvetta to get well? What can He say to that prayer?

May 7, 2007

This is not a good day. A young lady whose mother has been here for only a little time introduces herself to me. I tell her how wonderful Hospice is and that her mother and father will be well taken care of. This is at 11:25 a.m. The mother dies at 12:55 p.m.

Alvetta would not eat lunch. I could not wake her up. She slept. I know our time is running out. I spent most of the day watching Alvetta sleep and reading my board material from Owens Community College.

At three p.m. one of the nurses walks in and tells me that it was and beautiful day outside and that I should "go for a walk". It was in the 70s and the birds were singing. I walked around the building and it helped my spirits. I have to remember how well I feel after my workouts at the YMCA and try to do more during the day.

They came to pick up the young woman who just passed away. I tried to comfort the family but it is hard to say the right words. It also lets me know that my day will be here soon. What would I want people to say to me? It's so overwhelming.

May 8, 2007

This will be a long day. I have a board meeting at Owens Community College. I asked Audrey to make certain to arrive at 11:30 a.m. I got there early.

Alvetta and I did not have much time together this morning. She was asleep and I didn't want to awake her. She looked at peace with the world. She appeared to be in a stage of complete rest. I see no fear in her face. She really looked years younger.

As she lay in bed I got this nice feeling that I was in the room with a lady, even in her sleep. One can tell that this is someone very special.

The nurses and aides also understand this. They come in groups hoping she will awaken to say a few words. When she does it is as if she has made their day. They have to put her makeup on and decide what scarf and gown she will wear. I can tell they enjoy the time with her because they stay for a long time. From outside the door it always sounds like a party is taking place in her room.

I have to leave for my board meeting. It is so hard. I know I need a break. A change of environment. Something else to focus on. So, with Audrey's insistence that I go and with a prayer that all will remain the same while I am away, I take off.

I attend the meeting in body, but my mind is back at Hospice, on Detroit Avenue, with Alvetta.

A Mother's Love

Audrey's Story

How many women would invite their husband's adult child into their homes to spend a week, sight unseen, and welcome them with loving arms? This is the question I asked myself over 20 years ago when I met Mom for the first time, bedraggled and tired after dragging my excited sons through the airport for our first visit to Toledo. When my oldest, Nashid, asked, "What should we call you?" Her answer was "Nana", and a love story began.

Nashid enjoyed trying to match his wits at chess and Mom had the patience to try and teach him. Bayyan, the youngest, was still in his 10-year old loveable stage, and loved to surprise Mom with his gentle pranks. Ever the prankster, we found out that Bayyan had left his favorite candy in each of the Christmas nutcracker ornaments that Mom proudly displayed each Christmas. Each Christmas thereafter, Mom always had Bayyan's favorite candy ready, although I told him he could never, ever stuff candy in the toy nutcrackers again.

Even Na'im, my serious middle child, was overjoyed to find that here was a woman who would watch sports with him and was really, really interested in them. Knowing I was a single parent by then, Mom helped me keep the boys dressed—well dressed to the envy of their friends.

Through it all, Dad got to saying "She's more your daughter than she is mine, Al." That really tickled her. I think the biggest tribute Mom could have given me was the time she said that she wanted to adopt me. I knew she wasn't trying to replace Cathy, my sister who'd died many years ago. I knew she loved me for my own sake and for that I was truly honored.

I will have to share with you something, however. Mom liked to have her own way, and well, I can be ever so slightly stubborn at times. When I first moved to Toledo, I moved to a beautiful but small apartment not too far away from Mom and Dad. Somehow, she had talked the landlord into letting her into the apartment even before I signed the contract so that it would meet her standards when I arrived. She even talked the landlord into giving me the "sample" apartment used to show prospective tenants! I arrived to an apartment with matching towels, toiletries, and other items she'd lovingly placed throughout. She even fussed, "I scrubbed the floor of the toilet for you, and I don't even scrub my own—I have someone to do that for me!" To me, she was saying, "I love you Audrey."

When I moved from that apartment to the next, apparently, I wasn't packing up fast enough and got this premonition that I needed to get a move on. Five minutes later, Mom was at the door, telling me she had come over to help. I knew I was in for a rough night, because we'd end up packing "her way." About 11 p.m. that night, I told Mom it was time to go home and the landlord would give me time to move the remaining articles to my new apartment. After all, I was moving within the same complex. It was snowing like mad, and I had to go to work the next day. As I took my last bundle to the car, Mom showed up with another one, determined that I would I would put it in the car AND unpack my car that night. We struggled, pushing that box back and forth in the snow that by now was coming down so hard we could barely see. Neither of us would give in. She called Dad and said. "Talk to your daughter." I got the phone from her and said, "Come and get your wife." Neither of us could believe how stubborn the other one could be!

When I moved to my current apartment, I timed it so that Mom would be busy, but the movers arrived late. I literally moved across the street, so it wasn't a big move. After an hour I could tell that they weren't moving to Mom's standards. I told them that if they didn't want to spend another few hours rearranging stuff, they'd better rush it up or Mom would give them a strong talking to. You should have seen those men running across the street with mattresses and other large objects trying to get done before she arrived!

Mom and I always had some project going. A year or so before, we took a couple of watercolor classes. We sewed, crafted, went to events together and shopped. I thought I knew how to shop, but after an intense 4-hour session of trying on clothes with her, I knew who the shopping queen really was.

Mom said I had a trained eye and could walk into a room and see everything that was out of place, had been moved, or was odd, with just one glance. When I arrived in Florida that dreadful March, one look at Dad let me know something was wrong. He said, "Something's wrong with your mother." She said, "Something's wrong with your Dad." Something was truly wrong.

After her surgery, I told Dad to write down the medical term for Mom's condition and call it in to me. Glioblastoma. Once again as when my son Bayyan died, I poured myself into research. In a couple of week's time, I'd found and read every article and experimentation I could. I knew I could hope and grieve at the same time.

How she loved the grandchildren! Marcus, Amani, Micah, Amir, Johnathan and baby Andersen! I couldn't get photos of them to her fast enough. One of my last photos of her shows her cradling Andersen and beaming with pride.

Mom was ravenous while in Hospice due to the massive doses of steroids she was given and could watch food shows nonstop. As long as she could she would phone me and tell me about the latest recipe she'd seen and ask me to make it for her and bring it in. I never did. I was angry with the folks who brought food to her despite her uncontrolled diabetes, so I put my energies into cooking contests instead. She would forget that I hadn't brought the delectable dish she'd asked for and admonish me to hurry up to enter a cooking contest so that I could win some money for us to take a trip or something. She's say, "Get your hips over there and….."

Toward the end, I didn't want to share my last moments with Mom with anyone. I'd arrive at Hospice only to leave once I got to her door and found a crowd. I finally found that early Sunday mornings were the best time to visit. Often we'd sit, not saying anything, but reliving the love, joy and support we gave each other.

Today, I can still hear her telling me that the pants I bought don't fit, that I forgot to put out the soup spoons, or that I'm not using my talents to the best of my ability. So with heavenly eyes on me, I've started to "Getting my hips over there" more and more and enjoying life to the fullest.

Another Day with Alvetta

May 9, 2007

Wow! The rain! I know that some parts of northwest Ohio will have flooding. It looks like it will last all day.

My day at Hospice is about the same. I stop in to see our neighbor and am told she passed away at 4:30 a.m. My heart is heavy. I know in a few days my heart will be broken like my neighbor's husband. She was a wonderful woman and she put up a good fight. I wish that she and Alvetta could have been closer.

The weather is wet! A little cool! All I want is a sweater and a nice place to hide from the world. How many more times do I have to hear, "Are you taking care of yourself?" "Is she better", "Is she having a good day?" "How is she eating?" I know they all mean well but the weight of the same statements just piles up.

I could not wake Alvetta up when lunch arrived so I covered everything up for later. She finally woke up at 1:30 and ate a little. I tried to get her to talk, but soon realized that it was not going to happen.

Relatives and friends arrived before dinner. She opened her eyes but didn't speak. She ate a little dinner—Jell-O, sherbet, and a little fruit, but she did not want the rest. I got her to drink a few sips of water. For many reason this was not a good day. Gramps has taken his first kidney treatment and Nana has come to realize that the two of them need to go into assisted living.

What a change we've had in our lives over the last 13 months.

May 10, 2007

I call my sister and discover that my mother was taken to the hospital after her visit to the doctor yesterday for a routine checkup. My mother turned 91 in March.

I call Mama's doctor to check on her condition. My mother has Alzheimer's, heart problems and a urinary infection. He tells me that her status improved over the last 24 hours but that her age and health were not a good combination.

It was time for me to head for Hospice to check on Alvetta. Only God knows what's in store for us!

This was a good day for Alvetta. She was sitting up and joking with the nurses and aides when I arrived. She has company all day and laughed and talked with them. She ate a little lunch and even tried to feed herself.

She is in great form when a teachers show up to talk and bring flowers. They talked about students they all had years ago and are now finishing college. It is surprising that she remembers the names of the students and is in disbelief that they made it out of high school. Her mother and uncle arrive to see her smiling. This is good for everyone. By the time her dinner arrived, she was tired.

Dear God, we thank you not for months or days, but for great moments like today. We must learn to cherish each precious moment you give us with Alvetta.

May 11, 2007

Wow! Another great day. The weather is perfect. My mother will come home from the hospital today. Nana and Gramps will move into assisted living and Gramps is being released from the hospital. Now I am on the way to see Alvetta.

Flowers are starting to fill up her room for Mother's Day. As I arrive, I can tell she is going to have another good day. She is smiling and talking. She wants to go shopping. She wants to see all of the grandchildren. She hears voices of children in the hall and wants to know if they are hers. She is confused on where she is but she is in a great mood. The visitors start to arrive and it's too many women in the room for me.

Its lunchtime and Sister Mary, a Hospice volunteer, tells me to disappear for a while and she will stay with Alvetta, be her company and feed her.

So I take off and visit the nurses and other patients at Hospice and have lunch. When I returned an hour later, Sister Mary told me that Alvetta ate very well and told her that I did not know it but she could feed herself. Everyone laughed. She did, I was told, eat a little by herself, but had to be coached and helped.

Everyone is gone. The shifts have changed. We both fall asleep. The nurse has to wake me to get Alvetta's readings.

God has given me another day with Alvetta.

Dinner really looks good. Macaroni and cheese, canned beets, chicken soup and a small cup of fruit. This is one of her favorites and she eats about a fourth of her meal, which is very good these days.

After dinner I rush off to the graduation at Owens Community College. I know that the trustees, faculty and others will be asking about Alvetta. I can tell them that that Alvetta had a good day.

At home I start my prayer to God and ask for another day with Alvetta.

May 12, 2007

It's not as warm as yesterday and is lightly overcast. I make my calls to family to see how everyone is doing.

Hospice of Northwest Ohio has two locations in the Toledo area. Both are well located and the grounds are beautiful. Each patient's room has a view of the grounds. There are lots of trees, flowers, birds and open spaces but the real beauty is the staff that works there. It's hard getting ready to go there each day. But the staff makes it a lot easier.

Alvetta is sound asleep on this Saturday morning and I try not to wake her. The nurses tell me she did not eat much breakfast and she no longer wakes up as they enter her room. I do my job of moving things around and throwing out the olds plants and flowers. I get my book and sit in the big chair and waiting for lunch. I have to wake her up for 10 to 15 minutes before lunch so she will not fall asleep while I am feeding her.

It is hard to believe that the 13 months ago the specialists said Alvetta would not make it past 6 months. She is now close to 14 months. There have been a lot of slow changes in the last two months, however. There's been increased confusion, loss of appetite, a little headache but not to the point where I think the end is very near. Yet, I know she is dying. Everyone knows. They pray for a miracle. All I pray for is another day with Alvetta.

Closer to God

May 13, 2007

The sun is bright; it is a clear, cool day. It's Mother's Day. Alvetta's room is full of cards and flowers. I know it will be a full day for her. I mailed cards out to our mothers and Audrey. I didn't know if I would see them today. So they received their cards a day before.

I don't think Alvetta realized this was Mother's Day. She laughed with the kids and was happy to see everyone. She talked to Kyla. She did not focus on her cards and flowers.

I am glad that, even in this stage of life she is in, we were able to celebrate another Mother's Day with her. I am also sad as I know each holiday will be my last one with Alvetta.

It's good to remember so many great holidays of the past. The only way I get through each day is to remember all of the 51 years of celebrations of holidays and family gatherings.

Alvetta loved to entertain. The food for each gathering was always so good and plentiful. We would have to give it away or freeze it. We came up at a time when you could not throw food away. We would always have a theme for each celebration. Wow! All I pray for is another day with Alvetta.

May 14, 2007

Spring is truly here. By May 15 we would normally have had our flowerpots out and all the windows washed. The deck would have been washed and stained by now. The carpets would have been cleaned. We'd have a new bedspread on and would be making plans to travel and send out invitations for a cookout.

But instead I am at home getting ready to visit Alvetta at Hospice for the 162nd time.

The phone rang all morning with invitations from friends inviting me over for dinner on Thursday, the Toledo Mud Hens game on Friday and a poker game on Saturday. I am now accepting all invitations. It really helps me both physically and mentally to get out and be around other people.

It is time to go see Alvetta. The nurses gave her a bath and she is sleeping. She has on one of her new gowns. It is pink silk and she looks like an angel without worry. She looks so relaxed. Her fingers are so beautiful. Her nails are shaped to perfection.

The room is very quiet. The window is open to the soft sounds of birds singing. Alvetta seems to be smiling as she sleeps. It is a smile that is different from her normal one. I have noticed the smiles on her face for the last couple of days. It's as if she is smiling and talking to God. Even when I awaken her, her "new" smile remains for a few minutes and then disappears as the old smile returns. While she is asleep I fall in a very peaceful state. It is as if I am enjoying some of the pleasure that she enjoys. I can see and understand what the nurses were saying about being close to God at Hospice.

May 15, 2007

The weather is at an almost record breaking 90 degrees. The forecast is for storms and showers with a temperature drop of almost 30 degrees tomorrow.

Thank goodness for friends and family. Every time I feel down I receive the right card, the right call, the right invitation to dinner, a baseball game, an invitation for drinks or a care package. In the last couple of days I have received all of the above. It was at this time that I decided to go back over all the cards Alvetta and I have received since our ordeal and start to try and match them up on our down days.

I can tell that Alvetta's cancer is really taking over. She is more confused and talking to people who are not there. She is pulling at her sheets and staring into space. She wants to know who is in the room with us. The doctors and nurses and aides are looking in on her more often.

I find myself praying more. I am reading more motivational material as well as the Bible and information that Hospice has provided.

Shanon stopped by to cut Alvetta's hair. She could tell the change in her mother-in-law since Sunday (Mother's Day). Alvetta is talking but not on the same subjects we are talking about.

She is a fighter. She has beaten all odds to make it to this point. She and God will determine when she will leave us.

All I pray for is another day with Alvetta.

May 16, 2007

The weather turned cold from a high yesterday of almost 90 degrees to 41 last night and a high expected today of 61.

The doctor met me on my arrival at Hospice. She told me that they might have a hard time under Medicare to keep Alvetta as a patient. Her condition called for services that could be handled at a nursing home. Medicare may not continue to pay Hospice for its services.

This was a shock and I told the doctor, "Then Alvetta will die at home. I will not take her to nursing home."

Hospice will keep a patient up to 6 months—180 days. Alvetta has been here since December 3rd or 164 days. When she was admitted, we thought it would be a few weeks at the most. She has defied all odds.

I am very confused over my next move. What kind of help can I receive at home? Will my other insurance pick up the coverage? What kind of volunteer help could I get? The list of questions goes on and on.

Alvetta's condition will not improve. She will need more help each day with the smallest tasks and functions. I do not think a nursing home can provide the quality of service that I demand for her. She is a lady in her final days and I will make certain that she is treated like one.

May 17, 2007

I met with one of the Hospice social workers today. She explained a great detail about Medicare, Medicaid and other health insurance plans that cover all or part of the cost of Hospice care. She gave me a brochure that said:

> *There are two levels of care at Hospice of Northwest Ohio and may be the same at other Hospice centers. Acute care and residential care. For those who have acute care needs that require constant medical management, charges*

> *will usually be covered in full under Hospice insurance benefits. For those who are stable and receiving resident care, an out of pocket room and board charge is required. The conditions may vary from day to day; their care will either be classified as acute or residential on a daily basis.*

This is what that doctor was telling me about Alvetta. They thought she was stable and only needed residential care, but overnight she went back to acute and would need pain medications every few hours.

With the new medication, Alvetta is sleeping more and eating less. She is easy to upset. She thinks I am trying to force food, drink and medications down her throat.

I ordered good tasting soft food but after a few bites she would not eat any more. The same happened with her drink. She drank a little orange juice, a little water and that was about it.

I really miss our ability to talk a little each day. She will say a few words but that's it. I can feel the end coming.

May 18, 2007.

It is a very nice sunny day in the 70s. I was invited to an evening Mud Hens game. I had to take the proper clothes to Hospice because the temperature would drop to the low 40s at night. Today my mind drifted back to the birth of Cathy Yvonne, our daughter, who was born on May 19, 1956. That's another story that I may one day write about.

A couple of days ago the nurses advised me that Alvetta's new pain management care would cause her to sleep more. It's hard to believe that she can sleep any more than she is sleeping now.

The social worker I met yesterday told me not to be concerned about how long Alvetta is with Hospice. The nurses love her; she is a wonderful patient, and more than that, she is a lady. I could tell by the sound of her voice and the look in her eyes that she also has discovered what most of us know now—Alvetta is a lady!

Nana, Gramps and her Uncle Percy walked in late that afternoon at just the right time. They were so glad that she was awake and she was glad to see the three of them. She talked to each one for a few minutes. They all expressed how great she looked and how beautiful the flowers were that filled her room.

Percy pulled me aside to tell me that Gramps kidneys were operating at 30% capacity and he needed dialysis at least three times a week. The doctor is very concerned that he may have a heart attack or be poisoned by his kidneys.

Gramps is 92 years old and very stubborn. He can never again have the quality of life he once had. He has always been a free spirit, living life without restriction. He has not been feeling up to par for a long time. He is tired of hurting, wetting himself, forgetting and then getting out of breath with the very smallest task.

I am very selfish for a number of reasons. I do not want two deaths of the people that I love so to occur so close together. Second, the children need to know him more. Third, he has been my only father for over 51 years.

We have had wonderful moments together and one of the greatest ones was our trip to New Orleans. But that's another story I would like to write about one day.

Teaching Me Patience

May 19, 2007

This is Cathy's birthday. The weather is cool but the sunshine makes it a perfect day.

Those who don't believe in God should witness the birth of a baby or the dying process of a loved one. Over the last 2½ years my faith in God has increased with the birth of my grandchild and great grandchild. Through them we live on forever.

Today as I looked at Alvetta my mind drifted back to the birth of Kyla. The family gathered at the hospital where we were very lucky to witness her birth. I could see God at his best. We taped the event and each time I have watched it I feel my faith increase.

It may sound strange but it is the same with dying. The time I am able to spend with Alvetta each day helps me to appreciate life more and to hold precious each minute of every day. My faith grows stronger.

Being in the room with Alvetta for the last couple of months has taught me to be patient. To be quiet both in mind, body and soul. To read the Bible more and to accept those things over which I have no control.

Each day I pray and ask for another day with Alvetta.

May 20, 2007

It's another good-looking day. The telephone started ringing early. Friends and family called to be updated on Alvetta's condition. I did not want to go into great detail. I just told them know that she was comfortable and was still able to have visitors.

The Hospice parking lot was almost full when I arrived. Although there are only 25 beds, the parking lot is always over half full each day.

Alvetta's nurse tells me that she had just a sip of juice and a bite of bacon and eggs for breakfast. Another nurse tells me to let them know when I want time alone with Alvetta. This is their way of telling me her condition is deteriorating and I need to spend as much time with her as I can.

Audrey and Nana show up after church decked out in their big beautiful hats and Sunday best. This was Ladies' Day at Third Baptist Church.

Alvetta woke up for a little while and acknowledged them. She spoke a few words and went back to sleep.

Lunch and suppertime are getting harder. She is not eating or drinking. I try to get her to eat a little soup, sip a little water or juice. I try a little sherbet. She appears to not want to sip anything. She sometimes forgets she has food in her mouth. When not sleeping, her eyes appear to be staring into space.

I think each day now we will begin to see bigger changes in Alvetta. It's time to start to plan on the overnight stays.

May 21, 2007

Spring is now here, not by the calendar, but finally by the weather.

It's a slow lazy morning for Alvetta. She had no company until after 6 p.m. last night. While she was sleeping, I rested too. Even while she sleeps, I can still enjoy her company. I watch her face, listen to her breathing and it helps me to remember all the great days of the past.

Today my mind drifts back to our wonderful trip to Italy. It was one of those trips where everything went well. The weather, the tour guides, our fellow tour companions. We enjoyed the food, the wine, but most of all, we enjoyed the people of Italy and their beautiful country. We made so many friends on the bus that year that we still keep in touch with. It was also our last big trip with Dorsey and Tense whom we had traveled the world with over the last 40 years—that's another story.

At 4 p.m. Ric, Shanon and Kyla arrive. Alvetta wakes up. She has been asking about Kyla for the last couple of days. She was very happy to see them. She wants to sit up and talk a little. Ric and Shanon can see that she has changed in the last week. I can see the worry on their faces. They know she is dying.

But, we talk and laugh and Kyla, at age 2 is having a great time being the center of attention. They have a great playground for children at Hospice. Ric, Kyla and I head out to the playground and Shanon stays with Alvetta. This was a great stress release for me.

Another evening with Alvetta. After the children leave and it is back to our routine: she sleeps and I remember our yesterdays.

May 22, 2007

Last night I could not sleep. My mind was on Alvetta. She is not eating or drinking. Her eating habits have always been good. Almost overnight she has gone from enjoying her food to not craving anything. She loves her tea, coffee, juice and diet pop. Now it's hard for us to just get a sip of water in her. She really dislikes her meats and vegetables. She will only take a spoonful of soup and sherbet now.

She is now receiving her energy from a Higher Power than our earthly food and drink can give her. She is not watching TV. She is not reading the cards that are still arriving almost daily. She is not paying attention to friends, neighbors or family. Kyla brightened her up for a few minutes yesterday, but soon I will limit her visitors.

Alvetta's skin does not feel the same. The color is turning gray and the left side of her face is being pushed out of shape.

The doctor wants to change the way she takes her medication. Alvetta is refusing to take it orally now.

Through all of this she still smiles. For the first time in 170 days I left an hour early. Not because I had something to do, but I just felt the need to change my surroundings. To drive away. To escape for a few minutes being ever hopeful that tomorrow I will have another day with Alvetta.

May 23, 2007

It is another warm day in May. The skies are clear and the temperature is in the high 80s.

Walking into Alvetta's room brings tears to my eyes. She is asleep. The corner of her mouth has turned. Her skin appears to be a little gray. The food tray, left over from breakfast, appears not to have been touched.

I tried to wake her to say hello but she didn't respond. So I sat. I listened very carefully to hear breathing. Each day I can notice a difference in her breathing. Some days it is faster as if she is trying to catch her breath. Other days, like today it is so soft and slow that I watch her body for movement to see if she is still breathing.

The doctors, nurses and aides are very concerned about Alvetta and also about me. Each day they tell me to go play golf and they will take care of her. They will call if her condition changes. I know after all these days they will take care of her, but I can still remember the look in Alvetta's eyes that said, "Do not leave me alone."

I will not change my schedule. I will try to be there for her at the same time every day. I know that the end is close and rather than cut down on my time at Hospice, I know I will be increasing it.

May 24, 2007

Today was very warm. It broke the record of 88 by 2 degrees. A high of 90. It sounds more like summer than spring.

Today is just more of yesterday. I had to tell her friends not to stay long. Alvetta is not eating and is only taking a few sips of water or juice. Her sleeping has increased. She is very hard to awaken.

The doctor stopped by down and asked me how I was coping with Alvetta's deteriorating condition and the physical changes that are now taking place faster. I tell her it gets harder every day. I try to reinvent myself each night, but it is not easy.

I am making plans for the future, but it's very difficult to envision life without my partner of 51 years. I tell the doctor that I think I am prepared, but that I also realize I will soon hit a brick wall. I am very concerned on how my pieces are picked up.

This is un-chartered territory for me. I am a planner, but how do I plan for something like this?

Alvetta's afternoon was kind of a strange one. Her face became all aglow. She was smiling again in her sleep. She was at peace with this world. It was almost as if she was making plans to leave on a trip to another place. It appears as if she is ready. She is ready, but I am not ready. God, give me one more day with Alvetta.

The Dying Experience

May 25, 2007

The weather will be in the 80s today. Alvetta's father will take his kidney treatment. The family did a good job in convincing him that we would like to see him stick around for a few more days.

I called Nana to let her know that Alvetta's condition was worsening. The thought of a miracle is out of the question.

Alvetta had a remarkable day. She can still fool people if they stay only for a few minutes. She smiles, looks at them and maybe says a few words. Two of our godchildren came to visit. Nana, Diane, and Jill were there. They think she was having a great day. She had them laughing at one time and was telling jokes.

Each day a Hospice staffer or volunteer would tell me something that Alvetta had said which would have them laughing at all day. Such as, "You really can't sing" to someone entering her room thinking she was asleep and singing softly. "Are you trying to fool me?" as they put her medication into her orange juice.

To someone trying to match her scarves to her gowns it was, "Do you really know your colors?" "You are too young for a facelift." And the list goes on.

Today was a good day. I look forward to tomorrow.

May 26, 2007

I know after the way Alvetta felt yesterday that this will not be a great day. Audrey is going in to Hospice early because I plan paint the deck with my brother's help. It has rained so I don't paint but do other chores around the house.

It was 1:30 p.m. when I arrived at Hospice. Audrey told me that Alvetta did not eat anything for breakfast and very little for lunch. She was in a deep sleep. As Audrey left I knew that the day would be long and painful.

I would rather be alone with Alvetta now. I really do not like company. The dying experience is not something I want to share with others.

The physical and mental change Alvetta is going through is not something she would want others to see. I know soon I will ask the nurses to put out a "Family Only" sign.

The change in her mental capacity is rapidly decreasing. She now whispers with little understanding. Her skin color is turning gray. Her eyes, which I could always read and listen to, are now glassy and tearing.

She seems so relaxed and so into her own world or into a new world. In this new world she appears very happy. Yet, I don't want her to go.

God, give me one more day with Alvetta.

May 27, 2007

It's hard to believe that it is 14 months since Alvetta's operation in Florida. Today Alvetta has made it eight months longer than predicted. She is a warrior.

Sunday was a great day for Alvetta. Not too many visitors thank goodness. I am thinking very seriously about stopping the visitors. Her physical appearance has changed. She hardly speaks. She whispers when she does. Her breathing patterns are very slow and irregular.

I will talk to the doctors on Tuesday. I want to know when I should start spending the night with Alvetta. She is dying. I do not want her to die alone.

I can feel already the reality of life without my wife. We met as kids at 15 and 18, married as kids at 16 and 19. We really helped to raise each other and our family. We made all the mistakes a couple makes and then some, but we stayed together. Part of our marriage vows was "until death do us part". I guess the only thing can that can break us apart—for a while—is death.

May 28, 2007

This is Memorial Day. The weather is a perfect 80 degrees without a cloud in the sky.

My friend Jim had decided to get our flowerpots full of the flowers that Alvetta loves. So, for the past two weeks I have been buying flowers. Jim is a master gardener and helped me last year with arranging and planting flowers.

Jim wanted to do this at his home so I loaded up the flowers. I had dropped off the pots a week ago. And for the next three hours we worked on the pots. I then loaded them back into the van and went back home to unload. I put most of the pots in the front. The rest will sit by the garage until I stain the deck.

When I arrived to see Alvetta, she was in a very deep sleep. I talked to the nurses about her morning. She has not spoken all morning. She did not eat her breakfast and had only a few sips of orange juice. She went back to sleep after her bath.

This is so hard. This hurts so much but I still have so much to be grateful for. Almost 51 years. 14 months when it could have been 6. An increased faith. A better understanding of friends and family. The foresight to put Alvetta in Hospice where she has received the best of care.

So many people really care. Each day I get an invitation to dinner, a card game or a round of golf or someone wanting to stop by and clean the house. The help I have received is wonderful. My neighbor knew I was going to stain the deck so he power washed it for me.

This Monday I accepted Jim's invitation for dinner and cards. We had done the flowerpots earlier that morning.

The hard part now is not knowing what to tell people when they offer their help. I have a list of things that need to be done, but I let my pride get in the way. I know that I cannot do it all. So I need to let go and let others help.

May 29, 2007

I met with the doctor to determine when will be a good time for me to start spending the night with Alvetta. She said the signs are: withdrawal, big changes in eating habits, picking at clothes and sheets, and skin color changes. Other signs that will let us know we are close to the end are: glassy eyes, decreased urine output, irregular breathing, and a purplish tinge to the hands knees and feet.

Alvetta is experiencing most of these now. I will decide each evening if I should start to spend the night. I know once I start I will do it every night until the end. I also when determine when I will let only close family members in to see her. She is sleeping deeply with her mouth open these days. It is becoming increasingly harder to wake up for her meals.

Today she rallied for a little while. She smiled and was able to talk for a few minutes. She also reaches out more to make contact and will then hold my hand for a long time. She doesn't want to let go. It's as if she is holding on to me to hold on to life.

She is dressed in a beautiful red and black gown. Her face is made up. Her hair is brushed and groomed. Even with all the things that are going bad, she still looks good.

May 30, 2007

Alvetta has been in Hospice for six months. Medicare will not pay her bill. Our insurance company is checking into our request to see if she is covered. It really doesn't matter, as Alvetta will be at Hospice until the end.

May has not been a good month. Two of our neighbors have passed away, one just last night.

Alvetta was asleep when I entered the room. She was dressed in her African print gown and the nurses have her looking like the lady she is. The weather is really hot for spring. Maybe this is keeping people away from Hospice.

I am trying to get ready for my 24-hour stays at Hospice. It's going to be hard. For the last 180 days I have walked these halls. I have watched new patients arriving almost each day and then leaving with friends and families crying. I have watched the name cards on the doors for each patient change. I have met a number of the patients and their families.

Each family is different. For some it's a time to rejoice. For others, it's a time to cry. Each circumstance is unique. The ones who seem to hurt the most at the end are the ones that look for miracles right up to the last moment.

I am as prepared as I can be but I do not know how I will react when the time comes. The act of grieving, I am discovering, is unique for each individual. As I stated before, my process started over 14 months ago. It may never end. Only time will tell.

For those who do not prepare themselves, grieving must hit them like a ton of bricks. I know the family and I will go through hell when Alvetta passes away, but I think I've gotten them as ready as one can. I don't think they will take it well but it may cut down on the amount of depression that will follow.

Nikki picked up Nana and Gramps because Gramps has not felt like driving since he was released from the hospital. They have not seen Alvetta for a few days.

This is not a good day for them to see changes in their only child. The gown, scarf and makeup helped a little, but that lasted for only a few seconds. Then reality set in. Their daughter was dying. They couldn't look for any more miracles. They didn't think she would have lasted this long but she had.

Alvetta was not talking or eating. She did not appear to understand anything her parents were saying. I could see and feel their pain. They are now a part of her dying experience.

May 31, 2007

The nurses stop in Alvetta's room and want to know a little of our past. Each day they ask questions to get more insight into this wonderful lady. We talked about our vacations. The one they want to know the most about is our trip to Italy.

I told them I would rank it in our top 10. We landed in Rome for 16 wonderful days, traveled by bus and stayed overnight in great hotels. The people, the countryside, the food were all better than the tourist guide told us they would be. One of the best parts was the bus driver and the tour guide who knew and truly loved Italy.

The other part I would put at the top of the list was all the people on the bus from countries around the world. In that short 16 days we truly became family, but that's another story.

Jill is one of Alvetta's Red Hat members. She showed up at lunch to feed her. She has been doing this for the last two months. Today she left in tears.

Alvetta

Someday we all will die—we know that. It will come to the young, the old, the rich and the poor. It will come to those with faith and those without. It will come to those who pray and those who don't. We all know that someday we will die but we cannot accept it in ourselves or in others. We grieve for others and at the same time we grieve for ourselves because we know, one day we will face the dying experience.

A Real Lady

Jill's Story

I met Al (Alvetta) in the spring of 1995, when I became her neighbor on Glen Arbor. I was very impressed with the fact that no matter what time of day I saw her, she was clothed with matching shoes, styled hair, makeup and jewelry. She taught me that dressing well and doing one's hair and makeup early in the day made one feel better about oneself and gave a person a jump start to having a good day. I had sold my business that year and had become lax about my appearance since I was at home all day. I learned that Al was right. When I took the time to look good, I felt good. I've continued to follow that advice and it continues to work. I just don't have the matching shoes Al had for every outfit. That lady sure had a great collection of shoes!

Al taught me that "Real Women Don't Pump Gas!" I'm blessed with a wonderful husband who pumps my gas. But that motto means more than just pumping gas. It means being a lady at all times. In this day of equal rights, some women have forgotten their femininity. Al was equal to any man but she was the most feminine woman I ever met.

Al was shocked to learn that I wore an oversized T-shirt for nightwear. One Christmas she bought me a silk lace nightgown. I used to love pretty nightwear, but after years of being a single mother, I'd forgotten how good it felt to slip into a slinky nightie.

Al even got me back into using the dictionary again. I always loved words and the kids and I would look up new words just for fun. Al had a great vocabulary and used words with ease. She once told me her doctor had described her as "stoic" regarding some problems she was having. The word stoic sent me home to the dictionary!

In addition to loving words and reading, we loved to laugh. Al once said I should write a book about all the funny things I told her. Boy, did we love to laugh. Even in her last weeks of life, when I came to Hospice to visit or feed her lunch—we laughed. She was very independent and disliked having to be fed. We joked about the fact that I made a bigger mess feeding her than she would have done herself. Our laughing made the situation more bearable.

I had tried to quit smoking for years and while Al lay dying, she promised to pray for me. Every time I got the urge to smoke, I knew I couldn't let Al down. Here I was praying for Al yet her prayers, in her final days, gave me the strength to quit. I haven't smoked since she went to Hospice. I know I never will again because Al's looking out for me.

Thank you, Al, for this and so many other things you taught me. We'll always be friends.

Jill Sedluck-Fraczek

Holding On

June 1, 2007

Alvetta did not eat her breakfast and only a few sips of juice. For lunch she had a few spoonfuls of soup, a little sherbet and a small bite of fruit. She has had very little urine output all day, which is another sign that she is coming to an end.

I do not like the sound of her breathing—it is deep and sometimes I can hear a rattle. Her mouth is open now most of the time and she stares with glazed eyes. She tries to talk but it's almost a whisper and is very slow. I have to be close to hear her.

After all these days, people still come to see her. I know the time is near for me to put up the "family only" sign. It will be difficult. She will not want people to see her in her final stage.

One of the things I know will change for me in the future is listening to people who whine about everything—they will not have my ear. People do not know how good health and life are. They cry all the time: the politicians, the Democrats, the Republicans, the rich, the poor, the middle class, the news media—and you and I.

Maybe if we took this time to really enjoy life wars would stop. We should be glad that we are alive and celebrate life as often as possible!

Over the past 14 months Alvetta just wanted to live for special days, such as Easter, her birthday (June 12th, 2006), Labor Day, and Thanksgiving. She really wanted to see another Christmas. Then she wanted to live to see the Year 2007.

Now I think she wants to celebrate another birthday, just 11 days away. She will be 68 years old.

Some will say, "That's in God's hands." I think Alvetta has proven, at least to me, that she will decide when it is time for her to go. She has beaten all odds. They gave her six months, and then 9 months, then, "It will be a miracle if she makes it to 12 months". Well, she has lived past 14 months.

I know she is weak and is not eating or drinking that much. She is also sleeping almost around the clock. Even in her condition, she is still the bravest person I know.

Sister Mary, one of the volunteer nuns, came to sit with Alvetta while I took one of my many daily walks. When I returned, Sister Mary said Alvetta would not let her hand go. She had a strong grip. I finally talked her into letting Sister Mary's hand go.

She does this a lot. She grabs a hand and holds on. As weak as she is, her grip is very strong. It's as if she is holding on for dear life.

I am so glad the number of visitors is down. She needs her rest. I am having a tough time reinventing myself each day. I am now fighting sleep and am depressed. I probably need to see a doctor, but I want to wait and make certain I am here for her as much as I can be.

It is 4 p.m. and Alvetta's visitors are gone. She is asleep. She has this beautiful mysterious smile on her face now when she sleeps that could put the Mona Lisa to shame. She smiles as if she has a very special secret that she wants to share but cannot share with anyone.

As I watch her, she puts my mind at ease and chases all of my fears away. She is either dreaming or has started her journey to the other side. If she has, then she is at peace. Her smile tells me that everything is ok.

June 2, 2007

The weather is quite hot and in the 90s. Alvetta has been in Hospice for 183 days.

Alvetta has on one of her newer gowns. It's the same color as the bracelet that a patient made for her four months ago. The bracelet is red, green, blue and crystal. She has never taken it off.

One of my neighbors showed up as I was feeding Alvetta. She recognized her and smiled. The neighbor thought Alvetta was improving, but after a few moments she could see her decline. She sat with Alvetta and I went off to lunch. This was a good break for me.

Sitting in Hospice for at least 7 hours per day for 183 days—7 days a week can really be depressing. So, every little break helps.

I watched yesterday as two families arrived and said goodbye to their loved ones. The patients had passed away. Both had been at Hospice for only a few days.

This is a very serious problem their loved ones missed the care and positive end of life experience that Hospice is noted for. To think one must wait until the last possible moment is, at best, a myth. The sooner the better, I say.

I have watched too many come in and die within 24 hours and their loved ones tell me they should have made the decision earlier. I am so glad that Alvetta is here even though it has been 183 days. She could not have received any better care and Hospice takes care of the family.

This day has been a carbon copy of the last seven days for Alvetta. She seems to be withdrawing from us slowly, oh so slowly. Food that she once loved gives her no satisfaction now. Sleep seems to be her only enjoyment.

Her breathing is very shallow and I have to watch her very closely to see if she is breathing. Her skin color changes daily, sometimes it's a title red as if she has a fever; at other times it's gray.

She has endured so much the last 14 months. She has not been alone. Our journey started over 50 years ago. I know that I will be there in the end.

Each day I ask for one more day with Alvetta. God has granted me another day—how may do we have left? It doesn't matter. We have today.

My brother Robert and son Howard (Ric) helped me stain our deck. It has threatened to rain all morning. We started at 8 a.m. and were finished by 11 a.m. Audrey spent the morning with Alvetta.

I arrived at 1:30 p.m. Alvetta was awake but in her own world. Audrey said she ate a little lunch. My expectations for the day were not that great. I was prepared to spend the night.

After Audrey left at 1:45 p.m. Alvetta fell asleep. Her color wasn't good.

It had begun to rain with heavier rain forecasted for the rest of the day. I hoped this would keep people away. I think the best for her right now is to rest.

Alvetta

    I am only one person as I watch my wife fighting for her life. It is hard to understand why anyone would take a life. I think of war and the senseless killing of others is insane. To send young people off to kill other young people mostly by people who have never faced war—but that's another story.

    Alvetta is having problems with her left eye as if she has no control over it. I don't think she can see very well out it. Her legs and feet are showing dark spots. She is not accepting food or water today. She is sleeping more. I hope we make it another day.

(You're) Always With Me

I said to you, when I was young,
That I thought that you were wise.
And as I grew older, I still
Saw that in my eyes.

You were so wonderful to be with
And demonstrated things I need.
So I feel within my heart:
(You're) always with me.

We sang and danced together
You teaching me a thing or two.
But there were times when you asked;
(Son) What's that new thing they do?

Arts & crafts so fabulous
You've shown so many to see
You've even made apparel
That fitted me so comfortably.

Many lessons you've shown me
Through the many years
And absorbing it all up
It's your voice I still can hear.

So for this time, a short farewell
For you again, I'll see
And until that special day arrives,
In my heart (You're) always with me.

Howard (Ric) Moore

Time is Running Out

June 4, 2007

Last night at home I was having a time like I do most nights. Depression is starting to come more often and stay longer. It is harder to reinvent myself each day. I know that soon I will seek medical help for this debilitating awful disease. I don't want to center my time, mind and energy right now on anything but Alvetta.

The doctor thinks that her eye problems are the effect of the cancer. Alvetta has not awakened for me today. At 1:30 she is still asleep and hasn't eaten. The nurses came in at 2:30 p.m. to change her and her medication. I had to leave the room so I took my daily walk both inside and outside.

On my return, the nurses were gone and Alvetta was still sleeping. As I had walked the halls everyone had asked how Alvetta was doing. I just said, "Not too good".

Ric came at 4:00 p.m. as Alvetta was just waking up. She wanted to talk but we could not understand her. I know this is hard on him to see his mother in this stage. I tried to get him talking about other things but the look in his eyes told me of some of the pain he was feeling. He left about 5 p.m. just before her dinner arrived. She barely woke up to eat. All she had was a couple of sips of chicken broth and half of her apple juice.

I know my time is close to spending the night. Each day she is more disoriented and everyone is noticing the physical changes. I head for home with the strong feeling of hopelessness—which leads more and more each night to a real lack of sleep.

I know the family, friends and Hospice staff can feel the sorrow in my face each day.

I know the worst is yet to come but for now—God, thanks for another day with Alvetta.

June 5, 2007

The weather is wet, cool, and it has been raining for a few days with more to come.

Alvetta's room is full of nurses, nurse's aides and the masseuse. They have given her a bath and a full body massage. She is awake. She grabs my hand, looks me straight in the eyes and squeezes tightly. She will not let go. She finally goes to sleep so I can pull away.

The doctor and his medical students walked in and gave Alvetta a checkup. They woke her up so they could talk to her and look at her left eye. Alvetta did not respond to the doctor's questions and could not follow his fingers to determine how bad her eye was.

The doctor took me aside and said that she was really starting to decline at a faster rate than when he saw her a month ago.

This Glioblastoma has been a very slow-acting brain tumor. In the beginning I thought it would be very aggressive after treatment. I was told six months, but God is giving us more time. She has had a longer survival time than anyone could have dreamed of. She is an exception to the norm.

But now her time is running out.

The 3:30 p.m. shift had been off for a few days. They could see the changes in her and were telling me how sorry they were. At 4 p.m. I could see pain in her face so I told the nurse and she told me they would increase the dosage of medication.

I left 6:30 p.m. and in my mind I knew that was my last day going home until Alvetta did not need me anymore.

At 10 p.m. the nurse called me at home to let me know that the increase in meds had Alvetta back into a comfortable stage and she was sleeping peacefully.

I knew that sleep would be hard for me that night. I made calls to update family and friends. Then I took a hot shower and headed for bed not knowing when I would be back in my own bed again.

June 6, 2007

When I got up this morning, I asked the neighbors to watch out for my mail and papers. I know I will begin to stay overnight at Hospice.

Alvetta

What I don't know is how long. I do not take a change of clothes but do put my overnight case in the trunk of the car. I also have Alvetta's phone book. Every day for the last 186 days I knew this day would come. I was not walking the halls or the grounds as much as I had in the past. We had been blessed to have this time together, but I don't have to be a physician to know that Alvetta is preparing to leave us. She is eating and drinking very little. Physical changes are taking place.

I could still feel the prayers of so many and this had started over 14 months ago. They helped to sustain both of us as we left Florida, though all her treatment and ever after she was told there was no hope. They prayer kept coming and the blessing poured out. Now God has other plans for Alvetta and we must accept them. She has beaten all odds.

She slept nearly 100% of the day. Only for a few moments did she wake and take a few sips of juice. One of her nurses who are going on vacation wants to know if it would be ok to call back and check on her. It shows the love and respect they have for her. They all think she is special. I know that they look at all of their patients as special, but she is very, very special to them.

A neighbor wanted to see Alvetta for the last time. She told me that she would really miss her. She left in tears.

We all must die but it's hard to accept. I think I could accept my own death more than I can accept hers. I also know that when she passes a lot of me will die as well.

I had planned to spend the night. Alvetta's condition was slowly declining and I promised her I would be there at the end. Late that night, however, the nurses thought I should go home. Alvetta was comfortable and things would be ok tonight. So, I headed home full of fear, anger, and helplessness. These were the main emotions I was having problems controlling. At home the rooms seem to be getting bigger, the house colder, and the nights longer.

I don't like Alvetta in this condition. Sleeping, not eating or talking—just slipping away. She would not like herself like this. God, thank you for all of our yesterdays, but in this condition I will be satisfied with my yesterdays with Alvetta.

Blessed are those who mourn, for they will be comforted. Matthew 5:4.

God, Get Ready

Men are Not Supposed to Cry

> Men are not supposed to cry.
> Men can go off to war and die.
> Lose their loved ones and sigh.
> Why can't men cry?
> Do you show strength when
> Your eyes are dry?
> Today, tomorrow, go on and cry.
>
> JCM, 1981

June 7, 2007

Last night was long. I am ready to head for Hospice early. It is a beautiful morning. The high for today is forecast to reach 82 and the sky is blue and cloudless.

I know what to expect each time I arrive at Hospice. First, the warm welcome and the smiles followed by the deep concern for Alvetta, for me, and for family and friends.

The concerns are real. Each day I feel overwhelmed. There are times at the end of the day I find myself crying uncontrollably. I am also having this strong feeling of fear for the future. The worst past is I am trying to hide it from others.

Alvetta's room smelled like springtime with all of the flowers. he blinds are up and the sun has lightened up her room. She is asleep but still the center of attraction. She has lost weight but it only improves her looks. She looks like a person full of health and ready to wake up and take on the world.

It's at times like this that I re-experience vivid memories of better times. Today, I remember one of our vacations. It was a cruise. This time we left the crowd and took a taxi to a private beach in Bermuda and spent the day swimming, reading and just enjoying each other. Whenever we vacationed with family and friends we always planned some time by ourselves. I know most married couples want to get away from their partners. We would make certain that we had our own space, of course. We lived our lives together "our way".

The Hospice chaplain stops in to see me once or twice a week. We pray together and have very deep conversations. I enjoy sharing with her some of my emotions, concerns and fears. This really helps me and I know she walks away with more faith and insight.

Alvetta is getting weaker. She may leave us in another few days. I was telling one of the nurses that her birthday was on the 12th of June. Her answer was, "God sent her to us on June 12 and it may be the day He calls her Home." Wow! If one believes in God, and I do, this will help me with the pain.

Friday, June 8, 2007

Today is very hot with a storm on the way. The sky is very dark as if night was approaching. Alvetta is in her 189th day at Hospice.

Alvetta has been sleeping now for almost 48 hours. She is not eating, drinking or communicating. The nurses are giving her their full attention. The volunteers seem to know and are deeply concerned about Alvetta's condition.

The nurses are talking about her. The words are the same as day one. "What a beautiful lady, both inside and out." "I wish I could have met her years ago. She is someone I know I could have learned a lot from." "She is so lovely." "She can really make you laugh." "Very dignified." The list goes on.

Jill, June and Myra were in the room and agreed with the nurses. They explained to them and to Sister Mary that one could visit Alvetta early in the day and she would have on her makeup and be color coded right down to her shoes.

After today, I think the family will start to gather and tell her goodbye.

Around 1:30 p.m. the storm rolled in. Alvetta slept through it. Her mother arrived about an hour later. The nurse had just cleaned her up. Alvetta slept the entire time her mother was there. It was the same with her friends, uncle and Sister Mary.

It's late. Everyone is gone. It's just Alvetta and me. We always made plans to have time for just the two of us. That's the way I have to look at it now.

There's a change in shifts at Hospice and the new staff have been updated about her condition. I can tell by the looks on their faces that Alvetta has reached another stage in the dying process.

I had not really sensed a fear of dying from Alvetta. I know it is complex because she had a great love for living. She has accepted her fate and without complaint. he still has that little smile on her face.

God, get ready for Alvetta. She is on the way.

Sister Mary came back to say goodbye to Alvetta for the last time. She only volunteers at Hospice once a week and doesn't think Alvetta will be here upon her return.

I think Alvetta and God are now making the decisions on when she will leave us and if I know my wife, she is doing the talking.

After I left for home I had a feeling that things were moving along a lot faster. At 10 p.m. I received a call that they would be increasing her medications. Hopefully Alvetta would have a very peaceful night.

I thought I had better go to bed and try to get some sleep. Little did I know that this would be a short night.

June 9, 2007

At 12:30 a.m. as a new day begins, I receive a call that Alvetta is not resting well and that the nurses were checking with the doctor to see what to do. She did not think I needed to come in. But at 1 a.m. she calls back and the tone of her voice tells me to get dressed.

When I arrived I was expecting the worse. Alvetta's skin was gray. She was having hard time breathing and was very congested.

I did not want to call the family until I was sure of the condition. At 4:15 a.m. the nurse told me her skin was cool and getting cooler. I thought at that time I would call the family. Within the next hour, everyone I called was there. I had prayed that she would last until they arrived.

At 6 a.m. things did not look too good. Her mother started crying, followed by some of the others. I fought to hold back tears. It was not the time to lose it.

We all gathered around the bed, talking, praying, crying and hoping. By 7:30 a.m. she was showing signs of improvement. She didn't wake up, but we could tell she could hear us.

At 9:15 a.m. we got the news that Alvetta's father had been readmitted to the hospital with heart failure. So, the family decided that some would go to see Gramps and others would stay.

At 1 p.m. Alvetta was stable and I told everyone to go home. I would call if things changed. By 5:30 p.m. I had decided to spend the night. It was my time and I was somewhat prepared to do so. I ate dinner in the room with Alvetta so that I would be close by. I really did not enjoy the meal because she had not eaten for the last 72 hours.

One of the nurses rolled in a bed at 9:30 p.m. that night. I lay down at 11:30 p.m. and listened to soft music and the night sounds that Alvetta made. Each time her sound changed it was like an alarm clock going off.

By 1 a.m. I had gone into a deep sleep, which lasted until 5 a.m. I woke refreshed and ready to face whatever the day would bring. I waited. That was all I could do. I'd had some rest, a good breakfast and all I had to do was wait. So I did.

My worst fear is to be alone. Yes, I have family. I have friends, I have children but when one loses one's wife after all these years, one is truly alone. I have not experienced the full impact of how it is going to feel, but I do know that it is my worst fear.

June 10, 2007

Alvetta made it through another night. She was looking as if she could not make it another day.

I called Audrey to come and relieve me so that I could shower, shave and change clothes. This also gave me opportunity to take my Nana to the hospital. Gramps was in intensive care and I wanted someone to be with him.

It all worked out fine. It also sounded that Alvetta's father might be released from intensive care today.

I made it back to Hospice by 11:30 a.m. Alvetta had been cleaned and wore a fresh gown and makeup.

Even though she was cleaned and dressed, she now appeared to be at death's door. Her mouth was wide open. Her breathing was laborious. Even with the morphine she appeared to be in pain.

I think that Alvetta will make it to her birthday on June 12. I know she does not know what day it is. Knowing Alvetta as I do, she wants everything neat, in place and very formal if she had to plan it. She would plan to be around for her birthday—only a day and a half away. Nothing would ever match her pajama party birthday last year. This could be close.

She had a cousin come visit her. They grew up together and are very close. It was hard for him to see her in this condition. I was glad he was able to come up and tell her goodbye. I think she could hear him.

It is late evening and Alvetta is making strange noises. It seems that she cannot clear her throat. She was coughing very loud, hard and often. I called the nurse. They thought she was having problems with swelling and gave her medicine to help.

With each new symptom I fear it is the end.

It was hard to sleep in the room on the roll away bed. I got as close to her as the two beds would let me. Although I knew her deep breathing and strange gurgling sounds would keep me awake most if the night, I still wanted to be close for these last few moments.

Family and friends now know Alvetta's time is very close. They are telling me that "God has a place for her"—Let God's will be done." "God knows best." "She is going to a better place." "She will join the angels in heaven." I know they mean well. I know they love her. I know she is ready, but I am not.

The night nurse really had to work with her. The strange sounds were increasing. Her breathing was up and down. The nurse had been her only male nurse and told me what a wonderful lady she was. How she was so modest when he introduced himself to her and how he had a female aide in the room to ease her discomfort. "She is a wonderful patient," he said.

Just 24 Hours

June 11, 2007

Just 24 hours to Alvetta's birthday! I think she is going to make it.

I was up by 5 a.m. Alvetta was in the same state that she has been in for the last week. She is holding on. Yesterday her mother truly and finally accepted the fact that there will be no miracle.

I called Audrey to come at 8:30 a.m. I wanted go home, shower, shave, change clothes and pick up Nana. I knew when I left for home that Alvetta's time was short. I wanted her mother to be there. So, I rushed home to shower, change clothes and hurry off to pick up Nana.

I was putting my clothes on in a hurry and a strange feeling came over me. It was as if a heavy weight had been lifted. The room looked brighter. The telephone rang. It was Audrey asking me to hurry. But I knew the exact moment my Alvetta passed away. I rushed to her mother's house and told her Audrey had called.

On my arrival at Hospice I told Nana that I had to rush to the room. I knew deep down inside what I would find. Audrey caught me at Alvetta's door and said, "Dad!" "She's gone." My body shook. I lost complete control. Fifteen months of knowing what the outcome would be did not, could not, prepare me for this moment. Even the professionals or the religious leaders could not prepare me for this moment. Even my faith in God couldn't have prepared me for this moment.

I cannot think of another moment in my life that I had felt like this. I had lost a father, brother, daughter, grandson and a great grandson, but nothing had made me feel this way.

I felt so much pain and so little control. From my head down to my feet, everything hurt. If you don't believe in souls, let me tell you they do exist, because at that moment I could feel the pain in my soul. I knew I would never be the same.

I never again want to hear "John I know how you feel," nor will I never say it to another human being. My wife of almost 52 years is gone—gone—gone…

I wrote a poem when my daughter Cathy passed away some 26 years ago. Today I recalled it:

Why

God tell me why you make us cry???
Would it be easier to let all of us die???
Each day you take away another one we love
Without a reason to what is happening.
Are we meant to be puppets?
And you pull the strings?
Do you laugh when we come to an end?
I have often wondered if you really are our Friend??

We lost a loved one
Did you cry……………..
Or did you roar up
In the sky?
One day soon we come face to face
Prepare yourself for the human race.

JCM 11/24/81

Alvetta's Re-Birthday

June 12, 2007

Today would have been Alvetta's 68th birthday.

We have called all the family and friends. People have started to stop by the house with food, prayers, kind words and all kinds of assistance.

I am in another world. I have just lost a part of myself. The loss of my wife, friend and my greatest support leaves me wondering who I am.

I was ok as a caregiver, but now I must become a giver of care to myself. That is going to be hard. My self-esteem is shot to hell. Numbness has taken over. My physical, spiritual and emotional feelings have been damaged to the very core. I am an outgoing person, but now the idea of any social contact is unacceptable. Yet, I must somehow pull it together.

Alvetta would want the very best homegoing celebration. I do not mean an expensive funeral. I mean one done with great taste. One with elegance, sophistication and class that would reflect the lady she will always be to me.

So I have to pull myself together. I can hear Alvetta telling me what to do and how to do it. I just knew the funeral would live up to her expectations and will be a great tribute.

June 13, 2007

The family met at the funeral home owned by one of Alvetta's Delta Sorority sisters who really knew Alvetta and will personally see to it that the services would be up to Alvetta's standards. Audrey, Ric, Nikki and Alvetta's mother all help in the selections.

The next day Audrey and I went to St. Joan of Arc to meet with Father Hite. With his able assistance we were able to work out the details of the service.

The night before I had picked out the music from the "Lead Me, Guide Me" hymnal. We would use some of Alvetta's favorite gospel songs.

Lead Me, Guide Me
Blessed Assurance
Amazing Grace
We've Come this Far by Faith
How Great Thou Art

We asked one of her childhood friends with an excellent voice to do the readings. Our old church choir from St. Martin de Porres will join the choir at St. Joan of Arc to perform the music.

For those of you who know the workings of the Church you know that choirs take vacations in the summer. Only a few members from either Church would be available. I called one member that I knew from each Church to recruit others, but not enough of them were in town.

So, I called a good friend, Clarence Smith, who has put on gospel shows for the Greater Toledo area for over 25 years. I told Clarence my problem and gave him the songs we wanted and the two contacts at the churches.

His words were simple: "John, do not worry. I will take care of this. You have other things to do."

Later people would say, "That diverse Gospel Choir is one of the best ones I have ever heard. I know they have been together a long time". Little did they know that the choir had met for the first time that morning!

The funeral met Alvetta's standards. We left the church that day with everything in order. I checked and double-checked everything. Audrey checked behind me.

You would have to have known Alvetta to really understand why we checked the details over and over to make certain all of the details were right.

In matters like this all who knew Alvetta Yvonne Howard Moore knew that she was a perfectionist.

Happy Birthday, Alvetta

I Love You

John

Blessed Assurance

The words from this beautiful song were having an effect on everyone in the Church. I was so glad that I had chosen it for the closing song. The choir was joined by all present. The words from the third verse gave me a sense of peace for the moment.

And when I think, that God, His Son not sparing;

Sent Him to die, I scarce can take it in;

That on the Cross, my burden gladly bearing,

He bled and died to take away my sin.

Then sings my soul, My Savior God, to Thee,

How great Thou art, How great Thou art.

Then sings my soul, My Savior God, to Thee,

How great Thou art, How great Thou art!

I know that we all must die. *My* day will come. I hope and pray that I have Alvetta's faith, courage and strength when it's my time.

Each day, for the rest of my life, I will thank God for the seconds, minutes, hours, days and years, he allowed me to be with

Alvetta.

References

American Brain Tumor Association, 2720 River Road. Des Plaines, IL 60018.
www.abta.org

National Brain Tumor Association, National Brain Tumor Foundation, 22 Battery Street, San Francisco, CA 94111
www.braintumor.org

Hospice of Northwest Ohio, 30000 East River Road, Perrysburg, OH 43551.
www.hospicenwo.org

Brain Tumor Society, 124 Watertown Street, Suite 3H Watertown, MA 02472-2500
www.tbts.org

The *Prayer of Commendation*" from the Rite of Commendation of the Dying, Ch.6,p.207. **Pastoral Care of the Sick: Rites of Anointing and Viaticum.** International Commission on English in the Liturgy. Catholic Book Publishing Co., NY, 1983.

Lead Me, Guide Me: The African American Catholic Hymnal, GIA Publications, Chicago

Printed in the United States
125073LV00004B/328-405/P